SIMPROJECT™

A Project Management Simulation for Classroom Instruction

PLAYER'S MANUAL

JEFFREY K. PINTO, PH.D.

AND

DIANE H. PARENTE, PH.D.

McGraw-Hill/Irwin

Player's Manual for use with SIMPROJECT™
Jeffrey K. Pinto, PH.D.
Diane H. Parente, PH.D.

Published by McGraw-Hill/Irwin, an imprint of The McGraw-Hill Companies, Inc., 1221 Avenue of the Americas, New York, NY 10020. Copyright © 2003 by The McGraw-Hill Companies, Inc. All rights reserved.
No part of this publication may be reproduced or distributed in any form or by any means, or stored in a database or retrieval system, without the prior written consent of The McGraw-Hill Companies, Inc., including, but not limited to, in any network or other electronic storage or transmission, or broadcast for distance learning.

1 2 3 4 5 6 7 8 9 0 QPD/QPD 0 9 8 7 6 5 4 3

ISBN 0-07-248085-8

www.mhhe.com/simproject

The McGraw-Hill Companies

PREFACE

This simulation is a dynamic business exercise designed for students enrolled in courses that emphasize the importance of developing project management skills. Because the simulation is designed to offer instructors maximum flexibility, we have included scenarios that bring into clear focus project management challenges within a variety of professions, including new product development, process conversion, construction, and information technology development and implementation. As such, the simulation can be used in academic settings within schools of business, engineering, hospitality management, information and systems, and architecture. The simulation is designed to provide students with real-world experiences in managing the myriad variables that are routinely encountered in project management and decision making. Best and most important, the simulation environment offers students the unique opportunity to practice various components of project management—a hands-on, learning-by-doing approach that emphasizes active learning.

The scenario and rules for the simulation can be learned in a short amount of time: perhaps two or three hours. Among the benefits for instructors are the randomization factors we have included that allow the instructor to customize the simulation each time it is used. These effects are important because they prevent past students from passing along "the key" to successfully winning the simulation. Each time you set up the simulation, you have the flexibility to alter key decision parameters, select project scenarios that are most applicable to your class, modify resource screens, and so forth. The default project example represents a new product development, an important challenge in today's fast-paced business world.

Playing the simulation gives student the opportunity to work either as individuals or in teams in making a variety of important decisions. First, they must make personnel selections from a randomly generated human resource table. Each individual has strengths and weaknesses; for example, they may be technically proficient but interpersonally challenged! The human resources each team selects is just the start, however; once personnel decisions are made and the simulation project team is formed,

McGraw-Hill/Irwin

the students are expected to make a series of management decisions each period, involving training, management of team personnel (discipline, motivation, team-building and reward distribution), team member training, assignment of resources to project tasks, and so forth. Each period, these decisions are processed by the instructor and result in impacts on project budget, schedule, project quality (functionality), and stakeholder satisfaction. Teams are graded against each other and their relative ranking is established based on scores across these key project performance variables.

Another unique feature of this simulation is its web-based design and the use of a central server to process period decisions. Many simulations require students to hand in hard copy to instructors, who input all decisions and manage the simulation from their own PC. SimProject™ requires students to be responsible for inputting their own decisions, allowing the instructor to monitor the process, while still controlling the processing of each period in the simulation. All results are posted to the website, and students can quickly access their results without significant waiting time. The benefit to you as the instructor is to free up your time to focus not on the mechanics of inputting period decisions, but on the overall process of how students made decisions and their implications on project status.

It has been suggested that among the benefits of simulations such as SimProject™ are:
1) To allow students with different academic interests to make business decisions after considering the multidimensional aspects of the decisions.
2) To provide the opportunity for students to interact in organized team-based settings.
3) To allow students to practice their communication, leadership, and interpersonal skills.
4) To aid in developing logical and rational decision-making skills.
5) To introduce students to the various issues of quality, stakeholder satisfaction, schedule, and budget implications that arise from decisions they make.

We genuinely hope that you and your students find SimProject™ a valuable, thought-provoking, and useful component for learning project management. Too many current project managers continue to learn their craft through baptisms of fire, with minimal advance preparation. This approach is expensive to their companies and discouraging to these individuals. In the past, this approach was necessary because formal project management training was often lacking and options such as project simulations nonexistent. Fortunately, this need no longer be the reality. SimProject™ is a valuable new tool for training successful generations of future project managers. We wish you the best of luck and success with all your projects!

ACKNOWLEDGEMENTS

Following our original conceptualization of the SimProject™ project management simulation, its development has charted a long and complex course. Though both authors have had extensive experience in using simulations in classroom and corporate training settings, undertaking to create a new simulation on our own was a unique learning process. One clear lesson we learned over the course of this project was the absolute necessity of finding a willing and capable set of partners, equally committed to adding their value to the product. In this, we were lucky enough to work with a software organization, SM Consulting, Inc. of Baltimore, Maryland, who brought a remarkable combination of programming skill, dedication, and creativity to their task of turning our ideas into a reality. James Ropar and Ryan Rowe have been tireless contributors, and it was a pleasure to constantly observe their ability to take our suggestions and go not one, but sometimes two or three steps better.

The editorial and book development staff at McGraw-Hill, particularly Scott Isenberg, has contributed much in the way of encouragement and support for our activities. The editing work of Cynthia Douglas has also added tremendously to the final product.

McGraw-Hill/Irwin

TABLE OF CONTENTS

McGraw-Hill/Irwin

TABLE OF FIGURES

QUICK REFERENCE GUIDE

REGISTERING FOR THE SIMULATION

1) Go to website http://www.mhhe.com/simproject.
2) Register as a New User.
3) Use the Player Registration Code in the front of this manual and the Simulation Code from your instructor.
4) Select your User Name and Password for competing in the simulation.

STARTING A SIMULATION

1) Your instructor will decide on team sizes and number of teams.
2) Your instructor creates class simulation teams once players have registered.
3) Once all players have been assigned to teams, your instructor will release the simulation for pre-play which is resource selection.

RESOURCE PROCESSING

1) In this round, players will either receive a randomly generated project team, or the instructor will have the option of allowing them to competitively bid for resources.
2) In the case where the teams receive a randomly-generated project team, they can immediately proceed to the period processing stage.
3) In the case where the instructor uses the competitive bidding option, all resources are first randomly generated by the computer.
4) Simulation teams submit their bids for resources.
   At a minimum, each simulation team must include one team member in order to proceed into the project play. However, we recommend that each team has one member from each of the major categories. As an example, in the New Product Development Scenarios, each team should have one member from each of the

following functions: project manager, product designer, engineer, marketing manager, and operations specialist. Resource categories are different by scenario.

5) Resources accept a team's offer based on a combination of the monetary bid and the team's attractiveness. Teams that do not win the resources they bid on must resubmit bids based on resources still available in the pool. Winning bids are a combination of monetary bid and team attractiveness factors. The highest monetary bid still might lose the resource.

6) Your instructor will likely have to conduct multiple iterations of the resource processing cycle until all teams are populated.

ROUTINE PERIOD PROCESSING

Each team must engage in three types of recurring decisions: managerial decisions, resource decisions, and training decisions.

1) Managerial Decisions—These represent players' decisions regarding corrective or supportive actions they take with their simulation team members. Decisions can be intended to motivate, punish, or develop group cohesion.

2) Resource Decisions—These are of two types: a) decisions about resource reallocation and b) resource assignment. Resource reallocation occurs when the players decide that their simulation team needs to be reconfigured, through adding additional team members or removing current team members. Resource assignment decisions require the players to examine the project WBS for activities scheduled for the current project round. All activities must have at least one simulation team member assigned to them.

3) Training Decisions—These decisions allow the players to assign simulation resources additional training if necessary. Training can either be technical in nature (e.g., computers or project management skills) or behavioral (e.g., interpersonal skills). Training resources increases their ability to perform project tasks efficiently as the project progresses.

Remember: Each simulation team member can be assigned to 150% of their available time across the entire processing period although we recommend that you not assign over 100%. Do not assign them to multiple tasks within the processing period unless you adjust their work percentage assigned downward to maintain the 100% total level. Assignment over 100% results in significant overtime charges against the project budget and decreased efficiency.

DISPLAYING RESULTS

1) Once all players' decisions are entered, the instructor processes the round. The resulting output available to the instructor includes: group scores, group managerial decisions, and group training decisions.

2) Group scores are a combination of cost, schedule, functionality, and stakeholder satisfaction. Cost refers to adherence to budget, schedule refers to maintaining current milestones, functionality is a measure of project quality, and stakeholder satisfaction is a combination of internal and external (client) stakeholder satisfaction levels with the simulation teams' actions.

3) Teams are ranked in terms of overall scores at the end of each decision period.

REMEMBER!

1) Make sure you do not overassign resources within each decision period. You should aim for 100% resource usage for each simulation team member within each processing period.

2) You will have a set of unspecified management tasks to which you should assign your project manager. You will be penalized if you do not assign these management tasks.

3) Your decisions in the simulation always involve trade-offs. Decisions that cut costs may also negatively affect project functionality or stakeholder satisfaction. Make sure you always ask cause and effect questions before engaging in major decisions.

4) Read the scenario carefully. It will provide tips as to the critical issues and success factors for the project.

5) In the case where resource bidding is competitive, it pays to make sure you have plotted both a best case for acquiring your resources and fallback positions in case you fail to gain your first choice.

6) When you have been assigned a randomly generated project team, carefully examine the personal characteristics of each team member. What are their individual strengths and weaknesses? Use this information to make informed decisions about assigning them to additional training.

7) You can complete the decision round without accessing all four period processing selections: training, managerial decisions, resource selection, and WBS assignments. You may submit decisions when you have at least one resource assigned to each task. However, be sure to click "Submit Decisions" on the processing screen

8) Rework is wasteful and costs your project in terms of both budget and schedule slippage. Make sure you are aware of the effects of rework and devote sufficient decision making to keep the functionality and schedule in control.

9) The cultural background of resources for project teams impacts on cohesion and team performance. A diverse group is more effective than one with minimal diversity.

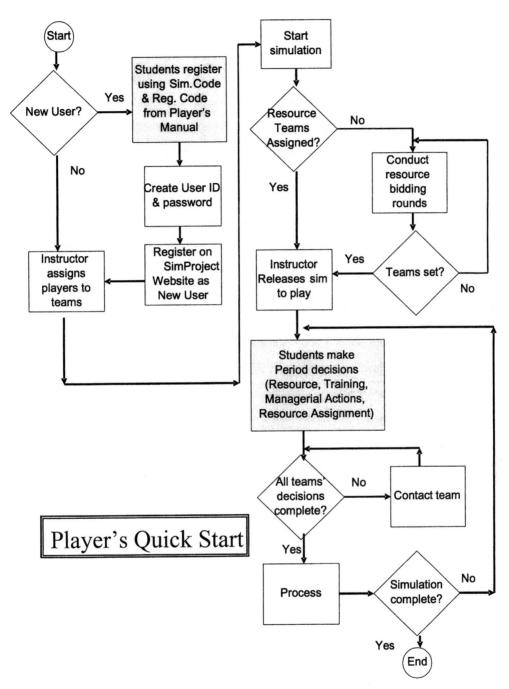

Figure 1 Quickstart Diagram

5

1.1 THE SIMULATION LEARNING MODEL

In the past several years, a number of significant changes have affected the manner in which we teach in the classroom. Research on active learning models, for example, clearly points out the advantages to students in terms of retention and critical reasoning skill development when they are given the opportunity to learn in an environment that involves them, offers problem-based approaches to learning, makes the process direct and active, and places a greater amount of the responsibility for learning on students. Students in an active learning model are more likely to be involved, to be engaged in the learning process rather than being passive recipients of information, and to employ higher-level reasoning and problem-solving approaches as they work in partnership with instructors to make their educational experience come alive.

Simulation offers one unique and valuable method for promoting active learning. Because it involves them in the "real world," requiring students to make decisions that are realistic and reflect genuine project circumstances, the simulation prepares students for the sorts of challenges they are likely to face in the workplace. Further, because decisions often have unexpected side effects or unintended consequences, the sooner students can be educated to think in terms of cause and effect, the better equipped they will be when faced with complex decisions on their own. Finally, simulations, to be effective, must force students to be reflective decision makers: to be proactive rather than reactive and to plan rather than respond emotionally or in a disjointed fashion. SimProject™ rewards participants who develop a coherent strategy for managing their project from start to finish, who plan their approach and stick to that plan. It specifically discourages the sorts of "hit-or-miss" responses that do not work in the workplace any more than in a simulation. These points are important because they offer your instructor the opportunity to create a unique learning environment for your class that can be specially tailored to your needs—while keeping learning active, interactive, and fun!

One truism of project management is that there is no such thing as a trouble-free project. In fact, research in the field suggests that many times successful projects are those that have simply recovered faster from delays and unexpected events than others that failed. One reason project management is such a challenge is because it frequently involves the need to quickly respond to unanticipated events or deviations from the original plans. SimProject™ incorporates this unique, but common, component of projects through an "unanticipated events" generator. Your instructor will have the opportunity at the beginning of the simulation to "sow" a series of unexpected events throughout the development cycle of the project, without your advance knowledge. These events, which range from the relatively benign (e.g., loss of key team member) to potentially catastrophic (e.g., project budget unexpectedly cut by 20%), cannot be anticipated by simulation teams but offer an excellent opportunity for you to learn appropriate responses that will have a minimal negative impact on your projects' development.

One additional, unique feature of SimProject™ is the direct linkage between the simulation and Microsoft© Project (MS Project) software. We have built in an access key that uses MS Project to actively track team projects, including all budget decisions, schedule status updates, and so forth. Consequently, an extremely valuable feature of SimProject™ is its ability to allow you to transition directly to MS Project, to use the software to track your simulated project, and become increasingly comfortable in using MS Project and understanding its multiple utilities. As a result, it is strongly suggested that student teams play SimProject™ in conjunction with networked computers that also provide access to MS Project. If you are playing the simulation using a stand-alone personal computer, please ensure that you have MS Project installed in order to gain the simulation's full functionality. A free 120-day trial version of MS Project 2002 is made available to you on the CD-ROM that accompanies this Player's Manual.

An additional feature of the link between SimProject™ and MS Project is the ability to save MS Project output files directly to your hard drive, using the "Save as" option when in the MS Project output screen. Once you have saved the file to an alternative location on your computer, it is possible to brainstorm alternative resource loadings, schedule lengths, and so forth, without adversely affecting the simulation-generated version of the output. You should note that you must still manually enter your decisions into SimProject™. You will not be able to upload your manipulations in the "offline" brainstorming into SimProject™.

It is strongly recommended that you recognize that simulations are only useful for active learning if they are approached with care and diligence. In practical terms, this means that you should seriously work to manage your project, just as though you were operating in a real work situation. Alternatively, when you try to simply "beat the game," you lose the opportunities for genuine active learning that simulation methodologies offer. As with any simulation experience, there are bound to be some rough spots early, as you become comfortable with the game. Keep in mind that everyone makes mistakes. Learn from them. Focus on these errors as a learning opportunity and a point of departure for playing the balance of the simulation. As you experience additional decision cycles, you will gain confidence in the processes and begin to recognize the links between project decisions you make and outcomes.

Even the best simulations cannot hope to completely mirror real-world experience. However, through the application of real-life project examples, coupled with links to MS Project and randomization options such as the unanticipated events generator, we truly believe that SimProject™ offers a significant advance over current simulation technology. Just as the best flight training includes simulators, SimProject™ gives you the chance to stretch your wings and fly, before you ever manage an actual project!

1.2 SIMULATION OVERVIEW

Managing projects represents one of the most important challenges we face in business today. The need to constantly balance the competing demands of diverse team members, top management, and customers requires project managers to work at a frenetic pace, to be creative, to exhibit leadership, use planning and organizing skills, acquire technical competency, and keep an eye always on the ultimate goal: the successful delivery of a viable project. Project management requires project teams to work to their best ability within constraints. The project has a limited budget, a fixed date for completion, and a defined set of deliverables (functionality). The goal of the project team is to complete the project while simultaneously responding to and satisfying all of these constraints.

Project management presents a number of challenges that are unique in business. Project managers must become not only technically proficient, understanding concepts such as scheduling, resource management, budgeting, and planning; they must also become adept at managing the behavioral side of projects—leadership, team development, motivation, goal setting, and conflict management. In this way, projects require the broadest possible set of skills from those charged with their successful completion. The "technical gurus" who cannot manage their teams will be no more successful than those who emphasize "soft skills" at the expense of planning and technical competency.

This simulation, SimProject™, has been developed to provide project managers and their teams with a realistic, comprehensive simulation experience that, as closely as possible, mirrors the diverse challenges and experiences you will face in running projects in your organizations. As players, you will work in class teams, making joint decisions, as you create and manage the performance of your project team, composed of personnel you will select, compensate, train, reward, and discipline over the life of the project. As a result, the simulation provides a dual learning experience. First, the simulation offers the opportunity to manage a project team through the trials and challenges of completing a project. The second challenge derives from the need to create and maintain a harmonious class team, composed of other students, who must develop a shared vision for project success and the most effective means for achieving it. Effective classroom simulations teach us exactly the sort of management skills that will become necessary in the business workplace: teamwork, decision-making, conflict resolution, organization and time management.

McGraw-Hill/Irwin

In playing SimProject™, all students start from an identical position. You (either individually or as part of a classroom team) have just been assigned to oversee the development of a new project at your company. You will either receive or be required to create a project team, and make a series of decisions every period as you move your project forward. You will compete with other project teams over a period of 12 decision rounds, where each round represents a set of project milestones. Your instructor may choose to play less than 12 rounds. Your challenge is to make the most effective decisions possible for each round, resulting in superior performance for your project relative to other classroom teams. Your goal is to complete your project with the highest score against the four project success criteria:

1) Schedule—All projects have a fixed schedule to completion. Time is a critical constraint for almost all projects. Your decisions must reflect the need to maintain the project schedule.

2) Budget—Your project has a limited, fixed budget as determined by your instructor and given in the Project Profile. Your score will be affected adversely if you overspend the budget. Team decisions must, as much as possible, recognize the need to keep project costs within acceptable levels.

3) Functionality—The project must "work." It is expected that at the end of the simulation, your project perform as intended, within the initially planned specifications. All team decisions should reflect the need to maintain project functionality.

4) Stakeholder satisfaction—Project stakeholders come in two major forms: external stakeholders, such as the customer for whom the project is being developed, and top management, who serve as an internal stakeholder for your company and must be kept happy. Team decisions should recognize that stakeholder satisfaction plays a strong role in project success and when making decisions, it is imperative that your alternatives recognize the need to keep stakeholder satisfaction levels sufficiently high.

To clarify the challenge of managing a project, think in terms of the project lifecycle concept, which identifies the key stages in the development of a project. As Figure 2 shows, project lifecycles generally move through four key phases relating to Conceptualization, Planning, Execution, and Termination. These distinctions will be extremely helpful as your team visualizes the status of your project and the demands and developments necessary to most effectively manage it across each stage. Note also from the figure that the life cycle evaluates project activity (usually measured in terms of man-hours) across the project's scheduled life. Life cycles help us understand resource requirements and budget expenditures over a project's life—extremely useful information to have in this simulation!

Project Life Cycle Stages

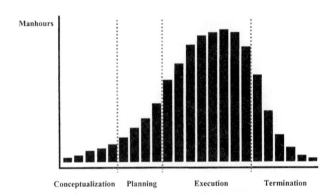

Pekka Rouhiainen
March 26, 2000

Figure 2 Project Life Cycle

- Conceptualization—The term refers to the initial goal development and technical specifications for the projects. We are trying to answer the questions: What is this project intended to accomplish? How will we evaluate its success? What are the key issues that we need to pay most attention to? It is during conceptualization that the scope of the work is created, the necessary resources are identified, and the important organizational contributors or stakeholders are signed on to the process.

- Planning—This is the stage in which all detailed specifications, schematics, schedules, and other plans are developed. The work packages are broken down, individual assignments are created, and the process for goal completion is clearly identified.

- Execution—This is the stage in which the actual "work" of the project is done, the system is developed or the product is created and fabricated, and other project-based activities are performed. It is during the execution phase that the bulk of project team labor is performed. As Figure 2 Project Life Cycle demonstrates, project costs ramp up rapidly during this stage in the project.

- Termination—In this phase, the completed project is transferred to its customer, the project resources (people, money, physical plant) are reassigned, and the project is formally closed out. As specific sub-activities are completed, the project begins to reduce in scope and costs decline rapidly.

These stages are the waypoints at which your project team can evaluate their own group's and project's performance. This life cycle is relevant only after the contract has been signed or the "go" decision has been made. It is signaled by the actual kick-off of project development, the creation of plans and schedules, the "work" of project development being performed, and the completion of the project and reassignment of personnel. When we evaluate projects in terms of this life cycle model, we are given some clues about their resource requirements. In this way, when we begin planning the project's life cycle, we are also acquiring important information related to lining up the necessary resources to accomplish the project's tasks. The life cycle model, then, serves as a combination of project timing (schedule) and project requirements (resources), allowing project team members to better focus on what is needed, and when.

Please Note: It is important to differentiate between the class team, to which you will be assigned, and the performance of your project team in the simulation. Your class team is responsible for creating and overseeing the performance of the simulated project team. Either you (the class team) will receive your team or select members from a personnel pool, add project team members or remove them, send them to training, discipline or reward them. The class team is expected to make decisions collectively that can affect the performance of your project team.

1.3 THE WEBSITE www.mhhe.com/simproject

The simulation is managed at a central server and can be accessed through the URL address: http://www.mhhe.com/simproject

During the simulation you will use the website to:

- Register
- Download the initial project scenario
- Enter your class team decisions each decision period
- Communicate with or post messages for team members
- Download end of period results, including Microsoft Project output
- Receive communications from the course instructor
- Explore tutorials and decision feedback
- Find answers to frequently asked questions
- Get help and technical support

SimProject™ requires students to have access to Microsoft Project in order to view the project plans. Microsoft Project must be available to the SimProject program either as a resident program or on a network.

The steps in starting up and playing the SimProject™ simulation generally follow this model: 1) setup, 2) project review, 3) decision making, 4) analysis, and 5) post project audits. Each of these stages will be examined in more detail in the following sections.

1.4 SIMULATION SETUP

The first time you access the SimProject™ website, you need to register as a first-time user. Registration involves the creation of a User Name and Password that you will use throughout your participation in the simulation project. To create the User name and Password, follow the "First Time User? Register Now!" link toward the bottom of the page. You will need the Registration Code found on the inside front cover of this Player's Manual and the Simulation Code provided by your instructor. In addition, you will be asked to provide personal data in "My Profile." Once you have created your User Name and Password,, there are a number of setup operations that you need to perform. We suggest that you first read the "About SimProject™" folder, which can be accessed from the opening window. Once you have read about the simulation, enter the "Player Central" site. You should enter your class team data, including the names of all members of your classmates assigned to your simulation team, in the "Team Profiles" location. You can add to or change team member information at this site using the "Edit team" and "Manage players" options.

The instructor will have access to all team member profile information and can verify that all team members have registered to play the simulation. Once the instructor has made this verification, you can move to the Project Review step.

1.5 PROJECT REVIEW

In the project review, all students must read the general project scenario, learning about the specific character of this project, its goals, constraints, and timeframes. PLEASE READ THIS SCENARIO CAREFULLY! The Project overview contains a great deal of vital information that can be a tremendous help in making decisions at each development step. Groups that thoroughly master the features of the project are in excellent condition to make informed decisions throughout the simulation.

1.5.1 Project Status Reviews

Among the key items to review are the initial scenario, the project Work Breakdown Structure, and the initial project schedule shown as a Gantt chart.

- Project Scenario—The scenario gives an overview of the project, its goals, important constraints (timeframe, budget, and deliverables) that must be accomplished in order for the project to be successful. The scenario represents your best guide to making decisions as you progress through the simulation.

- Work Breakdown Structure (WBS)—The WBS identifies the key activities, or tasks, needed to complete the project. Further, we have determined the stages at which these tasks must be performed, so you can begin to develop a sense of not only **what** tasks need to be accomplished for the project to succeed, but also **when** they need to be addressed. This information is critical as you begin to make decisions about resource assignments. You will find the updated WBS after entering the "Make Period Decisions" screen.

- Project Schedule (Gantt Chart)—The preliminary project schedule creates a time-phased plan to accomplish each of the tasks identified by the WBS. It also offers us the ability to link these tasks together using activity network logic. That is, all tasks are defined, as well as their predecessor and subsequent follow-on tasks. The advantage of a project schedule, such as a Gantt chart, is that it allows us to understand the affect that activities have on each other. If early tasks are late, it will negatively affect activities scheduled later in the activity network. The Gantt chart can be accessed under the "Make Period Decisions" link.

1.5.2 Requirements Review

All of this information helps us begin to assess our requirements for the project. The most important requirements, or resources, you will need to make the project succeed are people, or human resources. Therefore, one of the most important decisions your class

McGraw-Hill/Irwin

team can make is the selection of effective personnel for the project team. As you examine the WBS and the Gantt chart, you can recognize that certain personnel are going to be vital to completing the project. For example, in a new product introduction, design and engineering input is an absolute necessity. Likewise, having members on the project team from manufacturing and marketing would be very desirable, in order to gain the widest possible input to the team. Make sure that you begin to develop a sense for the resources you will need to successfully populate your project team.

1.5.3 Project Priorities Review

In reviewing the various elements of the project, make sure to pay particular attention to the project success criteria. While all projects are evaluated on the basis of conformance to budget, schedule, functionality, and stakeholder satisfaction, ask yourselves how these criteria conform to this particular project. Are some of these success criteria potentially more important than others? For example, in creating a new software product, you may feel that functionality and schedule conformance are key success criteria and focusing on these factors outweighs other considerations. Your project team's decisions should reflect this priority. Likewise, determine if there are other priorities that should guide, or underpin, group decisions. In situations where you face conflicts or obvious trade-offs, it is important that the class teams determine up front which priorities will guide decisions.

Your class team may find it helpful, prior to beginning to make period decisions, to conduct a goal-setting exercise. Once all team members have familiarized themselves with the project scenario, the other review documents, and project success criteria, begin to formulate a plan for how your team will work together to make consistent and appropriate decisions throughout the project. What are the goals that will guide your team? Are you in agreement on the key success "drivers" for this simulated project? Routinely ask yourselves prior to entering period decisions: Do these choices accurately reflect our perception of the key project success criteria? Are they consistent with the strategy you have chosen in developing and managing the project team throughout the simulation?

16

1.6 MAKING DECISIONS

The decision-making cycle consists of two parts: initial decisions and recurring decisions. The initial decisions that your class team must make concern assigning resources in order to construct your project team. Please note that it may be the case where your instructor has already randomly generated a project team for you. In this case, your primary concern will be with recurring decisions. Recurring decisions involve your class teams' decisions that must be submitted every period throughout the life of the simulation. You will make a series of decisions regarding resource commitment and managerial actions on a recurring basis.

1.6.1 Randomly Generated Project Teams

A feature of SimProject™ that is intended to streamline play is the random team generator option. Using this option, the instructor can instantly create a project team for each of the playing groups. The initial team is populated with the minimum number and type of project team members. As an example, in the New Product Development Scenario, teams would include a project manager, product designer, engineer, marketing manager, and operations specialist. Resource types are different for each scenario. Whether these individuals are senior or junior level, technically or interpersonally proficient, is purely a matter of random chance. This option mirrors the circumstance in many organizations when project teams are created and populated with personnel about whom the project manager has minimal input. When a simulation team receives their randomly-generated project team, they will then proceed directly to considering the recurring decisions discussed in section 1.6.2.

1.6.2 Initial Decisions

The initial decisions your team makes play a large role in your future success playing the simulation so they must be carefully considered. You will be expected to operate like a real project manager and bid for resources to populate your project team. Of course, depending upon how desirable the resources are, other class teams may also be bidding for their services. Therefore, it is important to remember: **resource selection is competitive and the approach you take must be carefully considered!** Consider your personnel choices and be prepared to pay them what you feel they are worth. If rival teams outbid you or have a higher attractiveness rating, you will lose your first choices.

When bidding for personnel, it is important to first make a preliminary determination as to how many and what type (function) of resources you will invest in for your project team. Remember that every person you add to the team is charged against your project budget, so your goal is select the best possible people, rather than simply adding large quantities of resources to the team. Also, all potential project team members you bid on are available to be bid on by your competition, so plan your bids accordingly. You may find yourself paying a significant premium over a team member's standard rate in order to acquire them. All personnel have a minimum rate as well that only your instructor has access to. You cannot bid less than the minimum rate for any team member.

Please note: You should populate your initial team with at least one member from each functional resource area. As an example, in the New Product Development Scenario, in practical terms, that means you will need to start with a team that contains (**at a minimum**):

1) A project manager
2) A product designer
3) An engineer
4) A marketing manager
5) An operations specialist

You will also have the limited option of choosing between senior level people (e.g., a senior product designer) and junior level resources. Your decisions to select either junior or senior level managers will affect both project performance (senior personnel work more efficiently) and your project budget (senior personnel cost more to hire). As the project progresses, your team will have the option of reviewing project team staffing assignments each period and either adding to or deleting personnel from the project team.

The initial decisions will likely require two or more iterations as teams submit bids and receive word of whom they have gained for their project team and whom they have lost to rival teams. After the first iteration, all teams should reconsider the Available Resource pool for their next set of bidding decisions. The initial decision cycle will continue until every team has populated their team to their satisfaction.

1.6.2 Recurring Decisions

After the teams have assigned the resources to create their project team, the instructor will "release" the game for full play. This release sets in motion the series of recurring decisions that form the bulk of the simulation competition. The key recurring decisions consist of: 1) Resource redeployment, 2) Managerial actions, and 3) Training.

1)   Resource Redeployment—The WBS and Gantt charts signal the class team as to the upcoming project tasks that must be completed by the end of the milestone. Resource selection must always be based on the types of activities that the project team will be facing. Remember that it is expensive to keep project personnel on the team if there are no specific activities for them to perform. Hence, the class teams should reevaluate the composition of their team at the end of every decision-processing period and prior to submitting their next set of decisions. If you determine that your project team is lacking members with important skills, you must acquire them. On the other hand, it you feel that keeping an expensive resource is no longer necessary, it is appropriate to release that individual back into the Available Resources pool. Remember, however, that added personnel will not be available for assignment to project activities until the next round, so PLAN AHEAD! Do this by paying close attention to the project Gantt chart and Work Breakdown Structure, as they signal the upcoming activities and offer

important clues as to the best types of functional specialists that can help the project move forward.

One important issue in resource redeployment has to do with assigning project resources to tasks. You will be asked to assign personnel to the upcoming tasks identified in the WBS. You will also have the option of assigning them at full time (100%), something more (up to 150%), or something less, such as part time (50%). Part time assignments make sense when you have two or more tasks that need to be accomplished but only one qualified team member to perform them. Remember that there is a tradeoff here: Assigning a team member to a task at 50% of their time will double the time needed to complete the assignment. Assigning resources at more than 100% will decrease their effectiveness and incur overtime charges. On the other hand, assigning them to multiple tasks on a full time basis ensures that you will be charged overtime rates against your project budget. It is important to look ahead, sometimes several steps, in the WBS to anticipate resource requirements before they become critical and begin adding team members to your project team in advance. Waiting until tasks are ready to be performed and then discovering that you lack a critical resource ensures lengthy project delays.

One final point: The simulation assumes that you cannot assign personnel to more than a total of 100% of their time over any decision period (usually indicated as work packages with milestones). Even when activities within a decision period are consecutive, it would be a mistake to assume that you can assign John 100% to activity 1, then 100% to activity 2, and so forth. As noted above, while you may assign personnel to more than 100% of their total available time for any decision period, there will be penalty in reduced efficiency.

2)   Managerial Actions—as the "boss" of the project team, your class team has a great deal of control over the performance of project team members. Further, because a key determinant of project success is the degree to which you can create a cohesive team out of a collection of individuals, many managerial actions are aimed at enhancing a sense of teamwork among all project resources or improving individual performance. Figure 3 Managerial Actions Screen, shows a set of

managerial actions that you can take any period, as well as their cost to the project budget. The actions can range from the small and inexpensive (sponsoring a team Happy Hour or throwing a Pizza Party) to the significant and expensive (holding a Team Retreat). The effects of these actions may consist of short-term morale improvement, speeding project activity completion, or they may be more long term, having no immediate effect but improving the climate for later performance enhancement.

Many managerial actions are routine, but important. For example, holding regular meetings with top management or customers are good methods for keeping stakeholders happy. Of course, the tradeoff is that meetings and many other routine managerial actions can cost your project team precious time. Like any other actions you decide to have your project team take, always remember to weigh the positive and negative consequences.

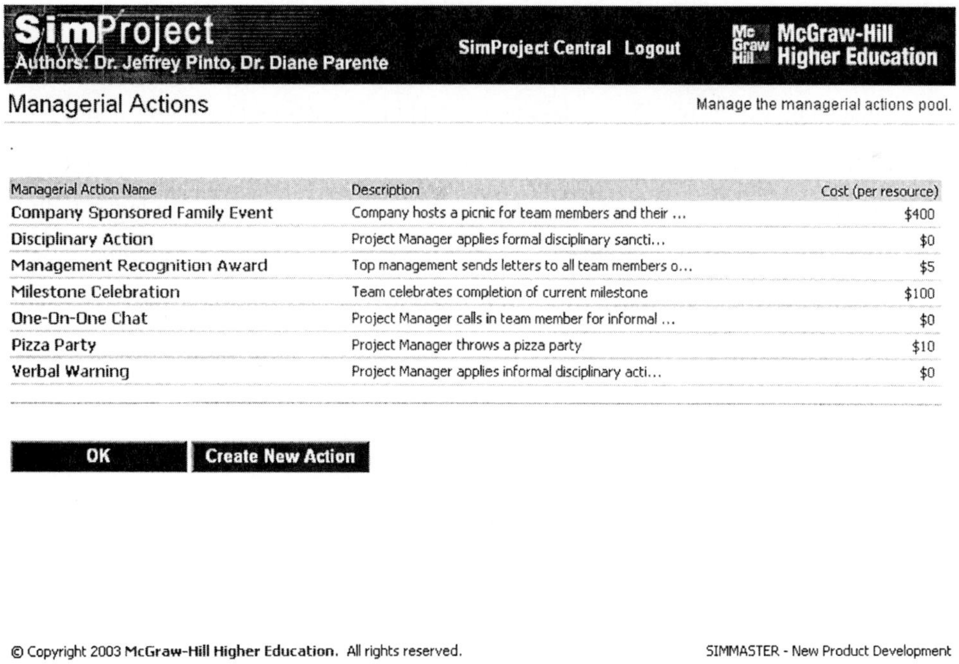
SimProject
Authors: Dr. Jeffrey Pinto, Dr. Diane Parente
SimProject Central Logout
Mc Graw Hill McGraw-Hill Higher Education
Managerial Actions
Manage the managerial actions pool.
Managerial Action Name | Description | Cost (per resource)
Company Sponsored Family Event | Company hosts a picnic for team members and their ... | $400
Disciplinary Action | Project Manager applies formal disciplinary sancti... | $0
Management Recognition Award | Top management sends letters to all team members o... | $5
Milestone Celebration | Team celebrates completion of current milestone | $100
One-On-One Chat | Project Manager calls in team member for informal ... | $0
Pizza Party | Project Manager throws a pizza party | $10
Verbal Warning | Project Manager applies informal disciplinary acti... | $0
OK
Create New Action
© Copyright 2003 McGraw-Hill Higher Education. All rights reserved.
SIMMASTER - New Product Development

Figure 3 Managerial Actions Screen

McGraw-Hill/Irwin

All managerial actions have an impact on team performance, either positively or negatively. Further, these effects may be immediate or delayed, short-term or long-term. As a result, some class team decisions may, at first, seem to have no positive effect; however, their effect may be felt over time as the project continues to develop. Also note that excessive managerial actions can lower project performance in the short term. If the team spends all their time having pizza parties, they are not performing to their capabilities. You will find that it is necessary to strike a balance between excessive and minimal managerial actions.

3) Training—Not all project team personnel come to your project team fully trained, with their complete set of skills. You will occasionally find that it is necessary to send away team members for advanced training in either technical or behavioral areas. They may need courses in interpersonal skills or advanced database management techniques, basic project management or conflict resolution. Training can have important payoffs but it also has short-term implications. When team members are training, they are not working. Also, training effects may be time delayed, so that immediate payoff is not always apparent. Training can also be expensive. Your class team must make reasoned decisions about project team member training. When should you use it? What types of skills need enhancement? Is it better to do it early and allow the project to lag initially, or wait until you get in trouble later in the development cycle? Make sure your class team considers these issues carefully prior to each decision-processing period.

In order to close the recurring decision cycle, you will need to formally submit your decisions. Make sure that you click the "Submit Decisions" button when you are finished with all of the Resource Deployment, Managerial Actions, and Training decisions (See Figure 4).

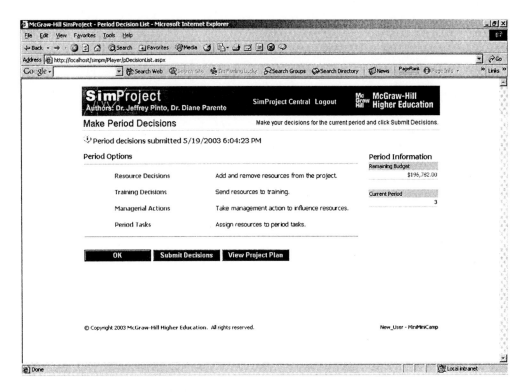

Figure 4 Period Processing Decisions

1.6.3 Decision Process Cycle

The basic steps in the simulation follow a sequence represented by these steps:

1) Instructor registers with the system for the new simulation.

2) Instructor configures the new simulation for play.

3) Players register with the individual Registration Codes.

4) Players are placed in teams by the instructor.

5) Instructor releases the simulation for Pre-play (allowing the teams to make resource acquisition decisions).

6) Players make bids for resources.

7) Instructor processes resource bids.

8) Steps 6 and 7 are repeated until teams are satisfied with their resource composition.

9) Instructor releases the simulation for Play (periods of decision making).

10) Players make period selections (Resources, Training, Managerial actions).

11) Instructor processes period decisions.

12) Players review results and make decisions for next period.

13) Steps 10 through 12 are repeated until play is complete.

14) Instructor ends game and generates post-project feedback.

These steps are shown visually in Figure 5.

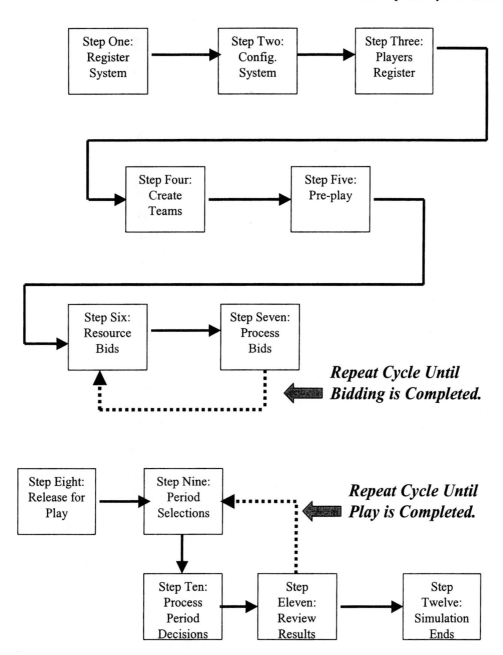

Figure 5 Class Team Decision Flow Chart

1.7 ISSUES TO CONSIDER

Making decisions on projects is a complex process. In trying to balance the multiple needs of keeping the project on time, on budget, on specification, and acceptable to customers, you will be frequently faced with situations in which you discover that these demands may conflict with each other. For example, in trying to keep the customer happy by agreeing to multiple change requests to the project, you can easily overrun your budget. In adding to the functionality of the final project design, you may find your schedule slipping further and further behind. In the real world, these kinds of project tradeoffs happen all the time. This simulation reflects the fact that you must always consider how your decisions will have extra (and sometimes unintended) consequences. As you play the simulation, you will be called upon to make a number of management decisions each period. To make the best possible decisions, you must always keep the goals of the project in mind. If the key success driver of your project is schedule, you should ensure that you prioritize your decisions so that the schedule is not negatively affected. On the other hand, many decisions can have more than one impact; for example, maintaining schedule integrity but angering the project customer. The complex nature of many of the decisions you will be required to make means that you should always consider their effects, both in the short term and across the complete project life cycle.

There are a number of issues and concepts that may affect a project in the real world. Prior to making decisions each period, your class teams must consider a variety of issues for your project, related not only to larger, strategic issues but also to operational decisions that will affect the performance of your project team each period. The set of issues that are relevant to your decisions include the following:

Alienating Top Management	Top management support may be lost if the project manager or team members do not act in a professional manner. It is possible to alienate, or estrange, top management by making repeated, similar mistakes, offending the customers, and so forth. Because their support is crucial for project success, you must ensure that your project progresses in a manner satisfactory to top management.
Impact Events	Impact events are situations that affect the project. The events may be short term or long term, expected or unexpected, and may or may not be related to the project. Impact events are not predictable. Project management involves the management of risk and uncertainty. Impact events may happen throughout the project as a way of mirroring that uncertainty.
Managerial Actions	As the project moves forward, your class team will have the option of using a variety of managerial actions to improve the performance of members of your project team. Some of the actions are coercive (disciplining poor performance) and others are intended to reward strong performance. Managerial actions can be applied to either individuals within the project team or to the team as a whole.
Top Management Support	Top management support is critical issue for project success. Support may be manifested in a number of ways, including supporting the team in disagreements with other departments in the firm, providing extra resources as the project progresses, and so forth. It may also provide an easier road to company acceptance of the project upon completion.
Rework	Project rework refers to having to repeat project steps or processes that were inadequately performed the first time. For example, projects developed by teams whose members have poor skill levels or lack of training are much more likely to require additional rework than better-trained and more efficient teams. Rework penalties include the charges for extra work at overtime rates and schedule slippage.
Stakeholders	Project stakeholders consist of all groups, both inside and outside the organization, that have an interest in or can affect the development of your project. Some examples of stakeholders include top management, other functional departments, cost accounting, and the project's customer. As your project progresses, one of your goals is to keep stakeholder satisfaction levels acceptably high.

Training Catalog	The Training Catalog consists of courses that are available to the project. Some of the training is behavioral (e.g., interpersonal skills) and some is technical. You may choose to send some or all of your project team personnel away for training during the project. Training your project team members may be both necessary and useful for enhancing their skills and project quality.

The simulation provides a great deal of information about each potential member of your project team. As you examine the resource pool, you will have the opportunity to consider a number of people for possible inclusion on your project team. As in a real organization, these individuals will have assorted strengths and weaknesses that must be taken into consideration when bidding for resources. Among the key issues that characterize the personnel pool are the following:

Individual	Cost/hour: Regular and overtime	Individuals have hourly costs assigned. The overtime rate will be some factor multiplied by the hourly rate. Remember that personnel costs are a large component of your project's budget.
	Education	Each individual will have a specified level of education that will refer to both the level and type of education completed. (i.e., B.S. in Engineering degree)
	Efficiency	Efficiency is the capability of an individual to act effectively. An efficient individual produces work with a minimum of wasted time, energy, or money.
	Experience	Experience is the length of time that the individual has worked in a specific area (e.g., construction). More experienced personnel tend to be more efficient and (at least initially) adapt faster to working on project teams.
	Reputation	Reputation is the general belief about an individual's character. It may also be described as the state of being well thought of. The better the individual's reputation, the easier it is to hire other team members, retain top management support, and keep stakeholders happy.
	Skill	Skill is the degree of expertise. Initial skill levels can be enhanced through additional training during the simulation.
	Training	Training is the amount of instruction in specific

		skills. It may be necessary to apply additional training to project team personnel if you determine it would enhance their ability to perform work efficiently.
	Work Ethic	Work ethic is the set of principles that individuals have about performing their job. A stronger work ethic means that the project team member is disposed to work more diligently.
	Flexibility	Flexibility is a measure of the adaptability of a person to a change in circumstance and the ability to handle changes.
	Public Relations	Public relations skills are the ability of a person to present an appropriate "face" to the external stakeholders.
	Interpersonal Skills	Interpersonal skills are those characteristics of a person to relate and interact with others.
Team	Cohesion	Cohesion is the degree to which the team will tend to stick together. Cohesion is a critical component in creating a well-functioning team.
	Efficiency	Efficiency is also a team concept and reflects the capability of the team to act effectively, with a minimum of wasted time, energy, or money.
	Longevity of core team members	Longevity of core team members is the length of time that the main members of a team have been working together. The longer team members stay part of the project, the more comfortable they are with each other, the better they understand the nature of their assignments, and the higher their learning curve. Teams with poor longevity suffer in their cohesion and efficiency.
	Managerial style	Managerial style is the way in which Project Managers conduct themselves with respect to performing the business of the project team. With respect to its effect on the Project Team, there are certain styles that will be more or less effective given the make-up of the specific Project Team.
	Team composition	Team composition is the make-up of the Project Team. Various factors will be considered in team composition including gender, diversity, education, experience, and training. Diversity can improve decision-making results but it can also lead to greater intra-team conflict.

Project	Cost: Estimated and actual	Project cost is the total time and materials for all costs associated with the project. Both estimated and actual incurred costs are important to project management.
	Functionality	Functionality is the degree to which the project operates in performing a specific task or operation.
	Milestones	Milestones are significant events toward the completion of the project. The project featured in the simulation will have between four and twelve milestones to completion.
	Project performance	Project performance is the degree to which the project fulfills the original objectives. The project's performance is measured on four dimensions: 1) adherence to schedule, 2) adherence to budget, 3) functionality (project quality), and 4) stakeholder satisfaction.
	Project profile	The project's profile can be described as the public face of the project. A "high profile" project is one that the company is investing its reputation and credibility in completing. It will command greater top management support but also greater scrutiny from project stakeholders. Your performance on high profile projects can quickly enhance or ruin your reputation in the company.
	Project stage	The project stage is the point of development of the project. The stage is usually associated with project life cycles.
	Resource allocation	Resource allocation is the way in which the individuals are allocated to tasks within the project plan.
Task Information	Time: Estimated and actual	Each task has an estimated time associated with it. The actual time will be determined as a result of decisions made in the processing.
	Prior performance	Prior performance is a measure of experience in performing specific tasks.
Project Management	Managerial actions	Managerial actions are specific events initiated by the project or organization management. These actions may be of two types: project management practices and specific events implemented as either reward or punishment for the team or team members.
	Managerial style	Managerial style is the way in which the Project Manager conducts him or herself with respect to performing the business of the project team. Their style can range from autocratic and disciplinary to team based and supportive.

1.8 ANALYSIS

After each period's decisions have been submitted, the instructor processes the decisions. You can then view the results of the most recent period. There are several forms of project output that the simulation generates, all of which are important for understanding your current status and deciding on future decisions. In the Player Central menu, select the View Period Results option (see Figure 6). This window will provide you with a wide variety of results from the past decision period, including: 1) relative team rankings, 2) training decisions, 3) managerial actions, 4) events, and 5) resource decisions. Other forms of output include a Microsoft Project file, giving the latest project tracking and control information about the status of your project. It is important for all student teams to become adept at interpreting project data from standardized sources, such as Microsoft Project. You will be able to access a number of screens giving information on schedule and budget status.

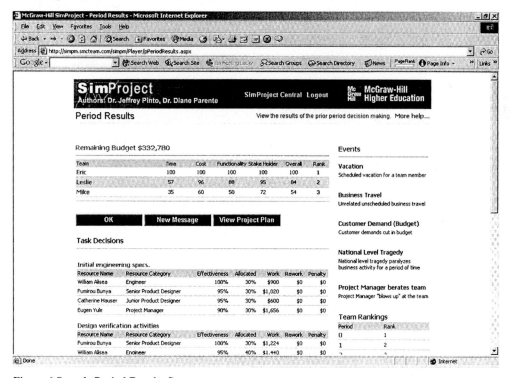

Figure 6 Sample Period Results Screen

1.8.1 Team Rankings

After each decision-processing period, the teams are ranked against each other in terms of their performance relative to the project success criteria of Time, Cost, Functionality, and Stakeholder Satisfaction. Using a perfect score standard of 100, teams will be ranked on a percentile basis and can compare their scores against the top performing class team. Your instructor will also receive a detailed feedback report indicating the impact that your period decisions had on each of the project success criteria. Team rankings can change from period to period as one team in the class outperforms their competition by making more effective decisions.

1.8.1.1 Time

A variety of issues can affect the schedule by which project activities occur. Although each team is evaluated against the same project schedules, the manner in which project resources are selected and assigned to project activities, the experience and skill of these resources, their motivation level and training, and the impact of rework can all serve to either keep the team on schedule or lead to significant project delays. The simulation evaluates dozens of variables resulting from resource decisions, training and managerial decisions, WBS decisions, and so forth to calculate the performance of your simulation teams relative to the schedule.

1.8.1.2 Cost

The amount of budget money spent in any decision period is a function of how much the simulation teams paid for their resources, whether they fully assigned them to tasks or even over-assigned them, and the overall variance the teams incurred (the difference between the planned rate of project budget expenditures and the actual rate). **Figure 7** shows an example of a project "S-Curve," the cumulative budgeted cost of work scheduled over the project's duration. Along the X-axis is the project duration, broken up

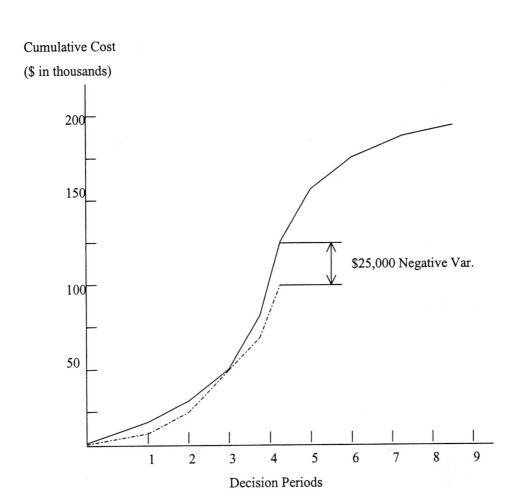

Cumulative Budgeted Cost

Cumulative Actual Cost

Figure 7 Project S-Curve

into the decision periods for the simulated project. The Y-axis shows the cumulative budget for the project. This example demonstrates a "negative variance," or difference between the scheduled budget of the project and the actual expenditures. A positive variance would show that actual project costs were outpacing planned budget. The simulation determines the expected budget amount to be used each period, based on the WBS and resources assigned. Positive variance, suggesting over expenditures, would lead to penalties to the player.

1.8.1.3 Functionality

The project's functionality, or measure of quality, is assessed by the efficiency with which project team members perform their operations, the relative absence of project rework, the assignment of the "correct" personnel to project tasks, and the skill level and experience of those personnel. The project's quality rating can increase over the life cycle as the players assign the optimal, trained personnel to perform project activities and support them with sufficient support as necessary. Excessive rework or assigning poorly trained or inappropriate resources to WBS activities will diminish the project's functionality.

1.8.1.4 Stakeholder Satisfaction

Project stakeholders are defined as any individual or group that has a stake in, can affect or be affected by the project's development. Typically, we can think in terms of two general types of stakeholders: internal and external. Internal stakeholders are those internal to the project organization. Top management, the cost accountant, other functional departments and their heads are all examples of internal stakeholders. External stakeholders are those outside of the project organization and the best example is the project customer, or client. A key goal of the simulation is to maintain strong links and positive relationships with both internal and external stakeholders as players develop their projects. Decisions made to either improve project quality or reduce functionality can also have significant effects on stakeholders. Stakeholder management is a juggling act, with many different effects on their attitude toward the project resulting from decisions the players make.

1.8.2 Training Decisions

The output report will also detail the training decisions your team made this period, showing the team members who were successfully trained, the cost against the project budget, and the number of days required to complete the training. It may occasionally happen that you will receive notification that a team member did not successfully complete a training program, requiring your team to determine whether or not to reinvest in training for that individual. The simulation will keep an up-to-date record of who has received training on your project team and the types of training they have undergone.

1.8.3 Managerial Actions

The generated simulation output records all managerial actions taken in the preceding decision period. Class teams can keep an updated record of the managerial actions they have elected to take and the personnel affected by these actions.

1.8.4 Events

Projects in real life never run smoothly. One of the real frustrations many project teams face is the fact that uncontrollable events can often intervene and derail a smoothly running project team, often at the worst possible time. SimProject™ was designed to reflect this uncertainty that all project teams face. The simulation, at the direction of the instructor, will sometimes generate a random "event" that can have serious implications on the project team's performance. For example, you may be notified that your project budget has just been cut by 10%, affecting your resource selection decisions for the next decision period. Or, the random event may suddenly remove a key team member, requiring going back to the available resource pool and bidding for a new person. You automatically lose any training or other positive managerial effects the reassigned individual had acquired. Remember: events are randomly generated and therefore, unpredictable. It would be costly and ineffective to spend time and budget money making excessive preparations for catastrophe in advance. Do your best to recognize the possibility of trouble spots looming without allowing yourself to become overly transfixed by them.

1.8.5 Resource Decisions

We have noted that your project team staffing must be constantly reassessed. Looking ahead in the WBS and Gantt charts to the tasks for the next period, ask yourself: Does your project team have the skills necessary to complete these activities or is it necessary to acquire additional resources? The output for each period includes a breakdown of resource assignments; this reflects both the adding or removing individuals from the project team.

1.9 POST-PROJECT AUDIT

At the completion of the simulation, a final audit will be generated. This post-project audit is intended to serve as a debriefing and critical analysis of each team's decisions and their impact on the project in terms of cost, schedule, functionality, and stakeholder satisfaction. Decisions on resources, training, and managerial actions all affect both technical and behavioral performance of the project. Further, random critical events and teams' responses to these threats offer some interesting discussion points. Instructors will determine how much feedback is directly provided to each team.

1.10 ORGANIZING YOUR CLASS TEAM

Experience with simulations clearly demonstrates that no team ever wins the competition by being "lucky." Successful teams are not just those teams that made the best choices; they are the teams that paid closest attention to how they would function. In other words, while the goal of this simulation is to bring your project in more successfully than the other competing teams, the best route to achieving that goal lies in paying strict attention to how your team performs. Two elements that you must take into serious consideration include issues of 1) structure, and 2) process.

The structure of your team is the manner in which you collectively determine that you will organize yourselves. For example, you may decide to elect one member as the overall team leader, with other people taking on supporting or expert functions. If your team is made up of people with widely divergent skills and backgrounds, analyze who can best serve to support the project in terms of helping with technical information, who can provide clues to behavioral issues, who has administrative experience, and so forth. Effective team structures may evolve over time, but they are rarely fluid. You will need to quickly settle into a structure that allows for maximum input from each member of the team. Look for each other's strengths and exploit them.

The processes you create can make or break your team. Processes refer to the manner in which you interact, your rules of behavior, expectations for community or appropriate behavior, and any other mechanisms by which your team will be expected to operate. For example, you may need to establish a set of ground rules or expectations early that emphasize your desire to make consensual decisions. Your team will function better once you create clear guidelines for how you will interact, punishments for inappropriate behavior, expectations that all members prepare and contribute equally, and so forth. Remember that in the absence of clear process guidelines for team meetings and decision making, there is a natural tendency for some members to dominate, others to withdraw, and still others to opt out of the process. Make your team expectations clear and make them early!

1.11 HELPFUL HINTS

Each time you play SimProject™ you will find that the results are different. Because of random generators and instructor options, the simulation can literally accommodate thousands of playing cycles and never replicate itself. However, just because the simulation differs in terms of key elements, it does not mean that you cannot learn from the experience. In particular, there are some helpful hints that will make your simulation playing experience more enjoyable and fruitful. Among the best pieces of advice we have gathered from past players, consider the following:

1) **Get organized early**—Organizing your team early on will definitely give you a jump on the simulation and your competition. Research and experience with simulations clearly shows that successful teams are invariably those that organized early and created clear structure and process guidelines. The sooner you get your class team up and running smoothly, the sooner you can begin to get your project team up and performing effectively.

2) **Read and then reread the manual**—The best way to win the game is to learn the game, thoroughly. You will need to read through this material and familiarize yourself with all the features, the various options, and alternatives. The more you know, the better prepared you will be to develop a winning approach. Every simulation debriefing has generated the same advice from those who just played it: "Read the manual."

3) **Develop a strategy and stick with it**—Consistency may be "the hobgoblin of small minds," but indecisiveness and changeability are worse. Make a plan for attacking this simulation and then work the plan. It may require fine-tuning, you may initially make some incorrect assumptions and alter your plan, but a consistent strategy is always preferable to simply trying a series of "hit or miss" guesses hoping to get lucky.

4) **Remember the law of cause and effect**—Every management decision you make is going to have an outcome, some good and some bad. Sending team members away for training will cost you money and lead to short-term delays. However, downstream payoffs can be quite large. Likewise, you may have to use discipline on some employees. It can negatively affect their morale but it may speed their productivity. Remember to think in terms of consequences. Also, remember that not every effect is immediately felt. There may be some time lags before the payoff becomes apparent.

5) **Think two steps ahead**—You have a project plan, including a WBS and Gantt chart. Use them constantly as points of reference to identify where you are in the development cycle. If you notice a task pending that requires a skilled person your team does not currently possess, go out and get them. Likewise, you can minimize current disruption to your schedule by early recognition of those in need of training and get them trained when they are least likely to have a negative impact on your project. For example, if you perceive that a programmer is weak in networking skills, the worst time to send him or her away for training is during the project stage when you need them to develop the networking protocol! Use the WBS to look ahead.

6) **Success lies in finding a balance**—Many of the decisions you make will have to balance competing and often conflicting demands. Remember, you have four success criteria: time, cost, functionality, and stakeholder satisfaction. You will occasionally have to make decisions in favor of one of these criteria at the expense of others. For example, to satisfy a stakeholder request, you may need to spend more of your budget than you would like. That is the nature of juggling competing demands. Unless you have a firm belief that one success driver strongly outweighs all others, be careful not to lose your sense of balance. All four criteria will determine your success. Keep an eye on them all.

7) **Be a leader, not a follower**—Success lies in charting a reasonable course, without paying too much attention to what other teams are attempting. You will know soon enough how your performance stacks up against theirs based on end of period output. Your best approach is to be original and independently logical,

without depending upon the other teams and the decisions they make. Yes, you are competing for resources and must factor that into your plan, but as much as possible, try and develop a clear and personalized strategy.

8) **Don't rush your decision**—There are a number of decisions that must be made each processing period. Leaving these decisions and analysis to the last minute puts your team at a great disadvantage. The sooner you identify your strengths and weaknesses, the sooner you can take corrective action. Making fast decisions is never a good substitute for making good decisions.

9) **Keep an eye on your budget**—Each team starts with the same project budget. Pay attention to how personnel selection decisions, managerial actions, and other uncontrollable events affect your budget. Using up the budget before the end of the project will incur significant penalties and forfeit top management goodwill. On the other hand, ending the project with significant budget money still available may signal a late project with client dissatisfaction. Find a balance between hoarding and squandering the project budget and review the budget status every decision period.

1.12 ALTERNATIVE STRATEGIES FOR STAFFING TEAMS

The first challenge you will face with SimProject™ is to create an effective team during the resource staffing phase. Recall that the random resource generator creates a set of team resources at the beginning of the simulation, all with varying personality profiles. Some are technically proficient but may lack interpersonal skills. Others have advanced degrees and skills, but come at an accordingly higher cost to your project budget. The manner in which you decide to staff your teams can have some important implications for how your projects progress. Among the alternative staffing strategies and their potential impact are the following:

1) Hire the best qualified and most expensive—Bidding for the resources with the highest qualifications will naturally incur a greater charge against the project budget. It is also more likely to provoke bidding wars with other players who also

covet these highly trained or experienced people. The benefits of adopting this strategy are that they allow you to acquire the top people to get a fast start, they cut down on training costs for the project, and these more proficient people can generally perform their duties more efficiently, with less likelihood of rework expenses or missing deadlines. The major drawback, of course, is that this strategy can be very expensive. These personnel are often in high demand and you should expect to pay a premium for these individuals to ensure you acquire them in the competitive bidding cycle. As a result, it is very important to keep track of the project budget in the event you choose this strategy.

2) Find the cheapest resources possible—The opposite of the first strategy is to actively seek to acquire the services of junior or lesser-trained personnel for the project team. Because these individuals are a smaller charge against your budgets, this strategy offers a low-cost alternative. Additional costs may be accrued in training over the course of the project, however, to improve the skill sets of these personnel. The major drawback with this strategy is that it will negatively affect the development speed and functionality of the project. Resources with lower skills cannot work as quickly or efficiently as those with better training and/or experience. Consequently, while this strategy represents a method to control initial budget costs, unless these personnel are given training to enhance their skills, the result will compromise project quality, schedules, and ultimately, stakeholder satisfaction.

3) Acquire "mid-level" personnel—A compromise strategy between the first two strategies is to seek personnel to populate your project teams that are perhaps not the best available but are a close second or third. The advantages of this approach are that it is less likely that you will enter into expensive bidding wars for these individuals, they can be trained to achieve proficiency fairly quickly as the project progresses, and they will do a good, competent job. While not the "super stars," these personnel will allow your project to progress at a reasonable pace. The disadvantage of using this strategy is that it may slow project development initially, until the additional training given these personnel begins to bear fruit.

4) Pay attention to a blend of both technical and interpersonal skills in creating the team—Effective project team members are usually those who have an adequate mix of both "people" skills and technical knowledge. We are all familiar with stories of highly trained but interpersonally inept individuals who adversely affect their project teams' performance through destroying group cohesion. SimProject™ recognizes the role that both technical capabilities and human relations skills play in creating a constructive environment for the project team. The greater the interpersonal abilities of team members, the quicker the team will attain high levels of cohesion, with a positive impact on the project. Likewise, the stronger the technical skills displayed by the project team members, the faster the project will progress, the better its functionality, and the less likely extra time and cost will be needed for project rework.

1.13 PROJECT SCENARIOS

In order to create maximum flexibility in playing SimProject™, we have created four common project management scenarios. These scenarios include a sample new product development project, construction project, Information Technology (IT) implementation project, and process conversion project. This section will briefly discuss each of these alternative project scenarios, giving a general overview of the projects, its goals and objectives, and significant milestones. It is crucial to your success in your simulation that you carefully read the scenario for the simulation you are playing.

1.13.1 New Product Development—D&J Plastics, Inc.

D&J Plastics is a 10-year-old plastics manufacturing company located in the Midwest. They specialize in developing parts for industrial use using injection molding and extrusion technologies. Their specific specialty lies in the area of developing made-to-order parts for the automotive after-market, although their product catalog includes products used within many industries, both marketed directly to consumers and those sold to manufacturers and retailers. D&J Plastics is a privately owned company with projected revenues for FY2003-2004 of $15 million.

In recent years, the company has begun to broaden its capabilities by developing design and engineering expertise in-house. This approach has allowed the company to expand its business opportunities by developing products for other firms that lack specific knowledge of plastics engineering and/or manufacturing. The impetus to expand in-house engineering capabilities at D&J has been identified by upper management as a necessary means for continuing to enhance business opportunities and revenue generation in this highly competitive marketplace.

McGraw-Hill/Irwin

The goal of D&J is to continue to develop in-house engineering and new product development to a level that will provide a sustainable competitive advantage for the firm over competitors in both the local and national markets. Recognizing the value of project management procedures, D&J has committed to improving their new product development through project management in the past three years. The company's objective is to re-engineer existing products and develop new products in a cost-effective manner while meeting customer needs. D&J seeks to use exclusivity agreements and patents to protect its revenue generation for these products.

1.13.1.1 Overview of the Project

D&J has determined that an opportunity exists to re-engineer a currently existing product known as a "slide." Slides are plastic hardware components that are used in automobiles to support drawers located in the driver's compartment, including dashboard and under-seat areas. The slide allows the drawer to be opened and closed. They come in sets containing four separate pieces, a runner and a mount for both left and right side. Research has shown that slides come in various configurations, colors, and lengths, depending on the application.

The project that D&J will undertake is to produce an 8-inch side mount slide commonly used for supporting dashboard roll-outs, including ash trays and cup holders, in Sport Utility Vehicles (SUVs). Various manufacturers are currently supplying this type of slide, both domestically and internationally, in a metal form produced by a roll forming process. The envisioned plastic product will allow D&J to offer a substitution for the metal version at half the cost to the automobile manufacturers. The target market for the slide will initially be domestic carmakers. Projected revenues from this project could come in as high as $5 million per year, making it a significant contributor to D&J's bottom line.

1.13.1.2 Connection to D&J's Strategy

Undertaking the engineering and manufacturing of the slide system for the automotive industry addresses several goals set by D&J Plastics. First, the company wishes to increase sales and protect revenue generation. Engineering a slide for use in the popular SUV market has the potential to generate large future streams of earnings. Properly engineering the slide can result in patent protection for the design, securing future product alternatives. Successfully demonstrating the viability of plastic slide components instead of traditional, more costly metal versions can open the door to future sales of plastic products in the automotive industry. Fourth, the project utilizes the existing expertise in the area of plastic part molding. Finally, the project can elevate the reputation of D&J as a plastic manufacturer and also as an engineering resource in product development

1.13.1.3 Objectives

The Slide Project has a number of identifiable goals associated with it. Its successful development and introduction will be evaluated against the following criteria:

- Budget—The project is budgeted at $500,000. The objectives require that the project cost total no more than 5% above initial budget allocation, without compromising quality or schedule to completion.
    - o On target—5% above budget projections
    - o Above target—Cost kept to initial projections
    - o Significantly above target—5% below budget projections
- Schedule—The project as a timeframe of 6 months (32 weeks). The schedule objectives require that the project be completed on time in order to exploit an existing market opportunity.
    - o On target—Project takes 26 weeks to completion
    - o Above target—Project takes 22 – 25 weeks to completion
    - o Significantly above target—Project takes less than 22 weeks to completion

Please note that the schedule can vary depending upon the instructor's modifications. You are able to consult the Gantt chart when you view your project for the exact schedule baseline. Should the schedule be modified to take either longer or shorter duration than the default 32 weeks, a good rule of thumb for assessing your project team's performance is to use the following guidelines:

- o On target—5% above schedule projections
- o Above target—Schedule kept to initial projections
- o Significantly above target—5% below schedule projections

- Performance specifications—The specifications for the project require that the team develop and produce a slide that meets technical requirements at lower-than-existing cost to current available products.

- o On target—Product is acceptable with minimal modifications
- o Above target—Product is acceptable as designed
- o Significantly above target—Product is acceptable for multiple uses

- Acceptance and use—The product is expected to capture 10% of the market within the first six months of release, while maintaining the desired gross margins.

- o On target—10% market share
- o Above target—11 – 20% market share
- o Significantly above target—More than 20% market share

1.13.1.4 Project Milestones

1) Computer-generated 3-D model of drawer slides
2) Physical sample produced from a stereolithography process
3) Finite elements analysis of slide structure showing compatibility of slides with existing models
4) Pre-production sample from temporary aluminum casting tool
5) Prototype testing approval
6) Final product and testing approval

1.13.1.5 Managerial Approach

The company decided to hire a new permanent Project Manager to develop this new product. The project manager will report to the President, and will have sub-contracted personnel as direct reports (see project team development). You will be responsible for staffing your project team. The decisions you make at this stage will have important ramifications for down-stream budget and schedule impacts on the project. You must make sure that monthly staffing costs do not exceed your current operating budget.

1.13.2. Construction—A Residential Housing Project

Hamil Home Construction has recently acquired a significant parcel of land zoned for residential housing and believes that the site offers tremendous potential for a large, single-family housing subdivision. In order to attract possible home buyers, Hamil have undertaken to develop the subdivision, including the construction of a single "spec" home on the property. They believe that once properly developed, with streets, utilities, and proper lot sizes, the property can be very profitable. However, the total project offers considerable risks, as well. The company will be paying for the entire development costs, including the cost of building the model home. As a result, their goals include the need to be as cost-effective as possible, as well as maximizing the speed of construction. Winters can be very disruptive to the building process in this part of the country, so Hamil is hoping to have the project completed before the start of the snow season (in approximately five months).

1.13.2.1 Overview of Project

The construction project consists of developing the infrastructure for the residential areas, as well as completing the model home within the five month "weather window" before conditions make further work expensive and difficult. The model home is envisioned as a standard, two-story, three-bedroom house, with attached garage and backyard deck.

The lot must be landscaped as well, to a minimum acceptable degree. Lot sizes are set for one-half acre, allowing for a total of 48 houses to be built in the development. Houses in this market are intended for upscale families (with one or more children) and listing prices will start at $185,000 for a basic model. With additional design options, floor plan changes, and interior upgrades, the "high end" models can approach $300,000. You will only build houses in this price range based on firm contracts, however, because the risk and carrying costs for expensive spec homes is considered too high.

The infrastructure necessary to support the housing development consists of grading and paving five streets, constructing sewer and water lines, extending telephone and cable lines along the streets, constructing the water catch basin, and surveying and grading all 48 residential lots. In addition, part of the land is heavily forested and will need to be cleared. Much of the infrastructure work can occur while the model home construction is under way.

1.13.2.2 Objectives

The construction project has a number of identifiable goals associated with it. Its successful completion will be evaluated against the following criteria:

- Budget—The total project is budgeted at $750,000 dollars. The objectives require that the project cost be kept as close to the budgeted cost as possible, without compromising building quality or appearing to "skimp" on the physical features of the development.
    - o On target—Costs kept to initial budget projections
    - o Above target—Costs 5% below budget projections
    - o Significantly above target—Costs more than 5% below budget projections
- Schedule—This project is operating under a significantly constrained schedule of 5 months (21 weeks). The schedule objectives require that the project be completed before the weather negatively affects construction.
    - o On target—Project takes 21 weeks to completion

- o Above target—Project takes 19 to 21 weeks to completion
- o Significantly above target—Project takes less than 19 weeks to completion

- Performance specifications—The specifications for this project require that the development's physical layout, infrastructure construction, and the model house be completed to a quality level that is consistent with the target market's expectations for functionality and appearance.
  - o On target—Project is acceptable with minimal modifications
  - o Above target—Project is acceptable as designed
  - o Significantly above target—Project leads to multiple advance orders for other construction before the end of the year

- Acceptance and use—The construction project is expected to lead to advance orders and down payments for 50% occupancy of the residential development within a two-year time frame.
  - o On target—50% occupancy (based on advance orders) within two years
  - o Above target—60% occupancy within two years
  - o Significantly above target—75% occupancy within two years

1.13.2.3 Project Milestones

Key milestones for this project include:
1) Zoning and surveying all residential lots
2) Clearing lots
3) Grading and paving roads
4) Laying sewer, gas, and water lines
5) Stringing telephone and cable lines
6) Digging model home foundation
7) Pouring cement and setting foundation
8) Rough framing
9) Electrical and plumbing
10) Wallboard, taping and plastering

11) Exterior siding and rear deck

12) Finish carpentry

13) Install appliances, carpeting, and flooring

14) Grade and seed lot, complete landscaping

1.13.2.4 Managerial Approach

Hamil Construction has decided to hire a permanent project manager to oversee the development of the residential construction. The project manager will have responsibility for both infrastructure development and the creation of the model home. As the project manager, you will be responsible for staffing your project team. The decisions you make at this stage will have important ramifications for downstream budget and schedule impacts on the project. You must make sure that monthly staffing costs do not exceed your current operating budget.

1.13.3 Information Technology (IT) Implementation Project

Auto Supply, Inc. (ASI), is a regional automotive part supplier whose business has seen steady growth over the past decade. With annual sales of $80 million, ASI has discovered that their information systems are badly antiquated. Communication between customers, suppliers, and departmental units is poor, relying on paper forms of communication (e.g., faxes, inter-office memos, etc.). While this approach was acceptable when ASI was a small organization, its increasing size and the complexity of its operations make the old information system out of date and a drag on the company's ability to grow further. The top management team has determined the need to develop a strong Internet and e-mail system, linking departments with each other and external stakeholders (suppliers, customers, distribution services) as effectively as possible. ASI's goal is to develop and install their new information system as quickly and effectively as possible, with minimal disruption to current work flows and rapid transition to the new technology by all affected employees.

1.13.3.1 Overview of the Project

ASI has conducted a preliminary project assessment to determine the key elements needed to implement the new internet-based information system. The project will consist of:

1) Research and needs assessment, involving interviews and systems analysis
2) Risk assessment and planning
3) Hiring an IT consultant to assist in the system design and configuration
4) Installation, testing, and debugging
5) Training and system maintenance for a limited after-installation period.

The project will require close coordination between ASI's management and the consultants in order to minimize disruptions to ongoing operations at the company.

ASI anticipates that the system implementation project will include a combination of hardware and software installation. Personal computers linked both internally and to the Internet, will be installed at workstations and personal computers throughout the company to link all employees. The project will require the services of consultants, software programmers, systems design and analysis personnel, and IT project management specialists.

1.13.3.2 Objectives

The IT implementation project has a number of identifiable goals associated with it. Most important in the minds of ASI's project team is the need to ensure that IT system functionality is optimized and stakeholder satisfaction is maintained at the highest possible levels. Their impression is that minor schedule slippage may be acceptable, provided the final, installed system is accurate, effective, and widely used by the company's employees.

- Budget—The total budget for the IT implementation project is $500,000, including the costs of software programming, systems analysis and design, hardware acquisition and installation, documentation and development, and consulting fees.

- o On target—Costs escalate no more than 10% above initial budget projections
- o Above target—Costs are kept to initial budget projections
- o Significantly above target—Costs are held 5% below initial budget projections

- Schedule—The schedule for the IT implementation project is approximately five months (22 weeks). Maintaining the schedule is desired, but minor slippage may occur, particularly if the installed system requires significant changes either during mid-project development or during debugging and testing after installation.
  - o On target—Project is completed with less than 15% overall slippage (three weeks or less)
  - o Above target—Project is completed with minimal slippage (less than one week)
  - o Significantly above target—Project is completed earlier than scheduled

- Performance specifications—The project's functionality includes an accurate initial needs assessment and creation of an Internet system that improves, rather than complicates, the operations of all employees. The system must be modified to suit the specific needs of the customers. Functionality is a critical success factor for this project, and great care should be taken to avoid trade-offs that can negatively impact on the performance of the IT system. Because post-installation change requests can be expensive and time-consuming, it is important that the implemented system conform as closely as possible to the user's needs.
  - o On target—Project is installed and used with nominal debugging and change requests (less than 10% decline in system functionality)
  - o Above target—Project is installed and can be used immediately with no appreciable time lost due to debugging and change requests
  - o Significantly above target—System offers additional features and options not requested but used by the customers

- Acceptance and use—IT system use is the critical determinant of project success. The final project must be widely employed and should, therefore, be demonstrably superior to current operations. Initial employee needs assessment and user training will be important steps to maximize the likelihood of system acceptance and use. It is our expectation that by all measurable accounts, communication and satisfaction among all system users will be maximized.
  - On target—System is used to 60% of its capacity by organizational members within six months of installation
  - Above target—System is used to 80% of its capacity by organizational members within six months of installation
  - Significantly above target—System is used to 100% of its capacity by organizational members within six months of installation.

1.13.3.3 Project Milestones

Key milestones for this project include:
1) Establish IT Project Management Team
2) Conduct organizational needs assessment
3) Hire external IT consultant
4) Develop project risk assessment and installation plan
5) Design and configure system
6) Purchase and install hardware and software
7) Beta test system with limited user group
8) Debug and reconfigure system
9) Develop system usage protocols and documentation
10) Train and monitor system users

1.13.3.4 Managerial Approach

While the essential goals of acquiring and installing a widely usable Internet system are fairly well understood, each project (and client) offers unique and significant differences

McGraw-Hill/Irwin

that must be addressed. The standard project management approach that ASI intends to adopt seems to make sense in that it provides a clear path to development and installation and addresses the key success factors for IT project implementation success. Your understanding of your challenges as the project manager makes it clear that the most important elements in a successful project will be your ability to maintain good relations with the system's users. Sometimes these good relations come at a cost. Customers in the IT field are notorious for being fickle with system characteristics; they like the opportunity to make change requests often and late in the development and installation cycle and they may not do an adequate initial job of specifying their needs. As a result, you and your team must work to balance system functionality and client acceptance and use with a fairly aggressive project schedule. You know from experience that this balance cannot always be maintained and the schedule can be prone to slippage, particularly if a poor initial job of user needs assessment was performed or if the project team ignores its link to the customer.

1.13.4 Process Conversion Project—Specialty Cups, Inc.

Founded in 1990, Specialty Cups, Inc. owns and operates ten injection-molding machines, which produce plastic drink ware. Specialty's product line consists of travel mugs, thermal mugs, steins, and sports tumblers. The travel mugs, thermal mugs and steins come in two sizes: 14 and 22 ounce. The travel and thermal mugs consist of a liner, body, and lid. The steins and sports tumblers have no lining. There are 15 colors that are offered, and any combination of colors can be used. The travel and thermal mugs have a liner that needs to be welded to the outer body; subcontractors and screen printers weld the parts together. Specialty does no welding, but it attaches the lid to the mug. Specialty's customer base consists of screen printers, distributors, and promotional organizations.

Specialty Cups, Inc.'s current method for producing its product is as follows:
  1) Quote job
  2) Receive/process order

3) Schedule order into production

4) Mold parts

5) Issue purchase order to screen printer with product specifications

6) Ship parts to screen printer for welding and artwork

7) Receive returned product from screen printer for final assembly and quality control

8) Ship product to customer

At current processing levels, the entire process can take from two to four weeks, depending upon order size, complexity, and the nature of current production activity.

1.13.4.1 Overview of the Project

Due to numerous complaints and quality rejects from customers, Specialty Cups has determined to proactively resolve outstanding quality issues. The firm has determined that by bringing welding and screen printing function "in house," they will be able to address the current quality problems, expand their market, maintain better control over delivery and order output, and be more responsive to customers. The project consists of adding three new processes (welding, screen printing, and improved quality control) to company operations. Specialty has no experience or equipment regarding welding or screen printing. The organization needs to educate itself, investigate leasing or purchasing space and equipment, hire trained workers, and create a transition from subcontractors to in-house operators. The project needs to have a specified date of completion so that the transition from outsourcing to company production is smooth and products can be delivered to customers with as little disruption to shipping as possible.

It is management's strategy that vertically integrating the organization will reduce costs, increase market share, and improve product quality. Specialty is currently experiencing problems with its vendor base, ranging from poor quality to ineffectual scheduling, causing Specialty to miss almost 20% of its customers' desired ship dates. Maintaining complete control over the product's development cycle should improve the quality and on-time delivery of Specialty Cup's product line.

1.13.4.2 Objectives

The process conversion project has a number of identifiable goals associated with it. Its successful completion will be evaluated against the following criteria:

- Budget—The total budget for the project is set at $125,000. Because the primary mission for this project is to conduct the process conversion in order to improve customer relations, technical quality is paramount. Budget slippage must be kept within reasonable limits, however.
  - o On target—Cost overruns kept under 10% of initial budget
  - o Above target—Costs kept to initial budget projections
  - o Significantly above target—Costs more than 5% below projections
- Schedule—The schedule for the factory process conversion is 11 months (46 weeks). The project goals require that the schedule be adhered to as closely as possible but not at the expense of technical functionality or customer satisfaction.
  - o On target—Project is completed with minimal slippage (less than 10%)
  - o Above target—Project is completed on time (based on initial projections)
  - o Significantly above target—Project is completed earlier than schedule projections
- Performance specifications—The specifications for this project require that Specialty Cups, Inc. bring three new processes in house: welding, screen printing, and quality control. Technical training will also be necessary to allow personnel to make optimal use of new equipment in order that Specialty accrue maximum returns from the process conversion investment. Clearly, performance (in the form of quality and functionality) is a key success factor for this project.
  - o On target—Conversion is completed and dependence on subcontracted screen printing is reduced by 60% within six months
  - o Above target—Conversion is completed and dependence on subcontracted screen printing is reduced by 80% within six months

- o Significantly above target—Project is completed and dependence on subcontracted screen printing is eliminated within six months
- Stakeholder satisfaction—The results of the process conversion should strongly affect customer relations through a decrease in product returns and improvement in delivery schedules while maintaining competitive prices. Since the goal of the process conversion is to improve stakeholder satisfaction, this factor is critical to project success.
  - o On target—Decrease customer rejects by 10% and reduce waiting time by 10%
  - o Above target—Decrease customer rejects by 20% and reduce waiting time by 20%
  - o Significantly above target—Decrease customer rejects by 30% and reduce waiting time by 30%

1.13.4.3 Milestones

Key milestones for this project include:
1) Technical approval
2) Select equipment vendors
3) Administrative approval
4) Plant layout redesign
5) Equipment installation
6) Employee training
7) Supplier selection
8) Develop inventory
9) Prototype with vendors
10) Prototype with customers
11) Customer approval
12) Project close-out

1.13.4.4 Managerial Approach

The equipment will be purchased from outside vendors; however, Specialty Cup's internal employees will perform the assembly work. Due to the type of equipment that is required, outside contractors will not be needed because the company's facility employs the necessary maintenance staff to set up the equipment and troubleshoot as required after the initial training has been supplied by the vendor. It is important to factor the cost of training personnel to operate equipment into the schedule. The goals of the project are clear: move assembly processes in-house to improve customer satisfaction and product quality.

2.0 PLAYING THE SIMULATION

2.1 Overview

This Player's Manual illustrates how players can use the SimProject™ online simulation software, including general usage of the software and detailed information about playing a simulation. This guide describes the software from the Player's perspective.

2.2 Registering with SimProjectTM

The first step for using SimProject™ by either the Instructor or the Player is to register with the simulation. To do this, you will need two codes: the Registration Code, and the Simulation Code. Your unique Registration Code can be found in the front of this Player's Manual. This is a unique nine-digit code in the following format **XXX-XXX-XXX** and is required to use the SimProject™ software. Instructors, during the creation of a simulation, generate the seven-digit Simulation Code, which they must distribute to their players.

To register with SimProject™

1) Go to http://www.mhhe.com/simproject. Figure 8 depicts the SimProject™ Home Page.

2) Click on "Register Now!" Figure 9 depicts the Registration Code screen.

3) Enter the nine-digit Registration Code found on the inside front cover of this Player's Manual, followed by the seven-digit Simulation Code provided by your instructor. Click the "Continue" button. Figure 10 depicts the registration screen.

4) Enter the required information into the registration screen and click the "OK" button. You are now ready to begin a simulation. See Creating and Modifying a Simulation for more information.

McGraw-Hill/Irwin

5) The process just described will result in your personal User Name and Password, which you will use throughout your class to access the simulation.

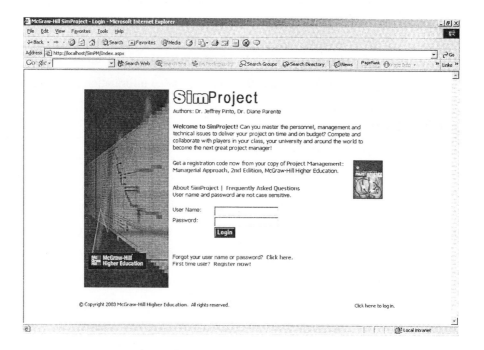

Figure 8 SimProject™ Home Page

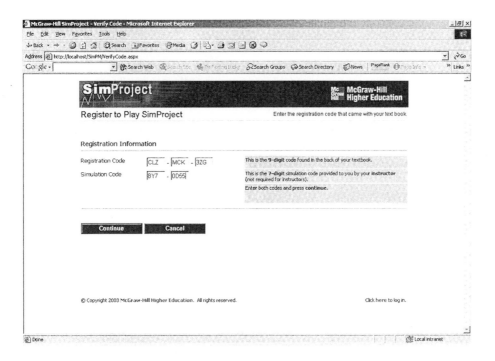

Figure 9 Registration Code Screen

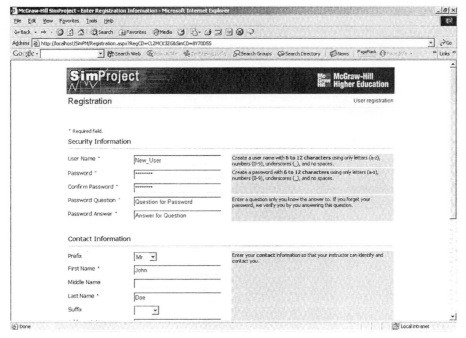

Figure 10 Registration Screen

McGraw-Hill/Irwin

2.3 Logging In and Out of SimProject™

During the registration process, you created a User Name and Password. These are required to log in and use the SimProject™ software and protect against misuse of the system. It is recommended that you log out of SimProject™ upon completing your session.

To Log In to SimProject™:

1) Go to http://www.mhhe.com/simproject. Figure 11 depicts the SimProject™ Home Page.

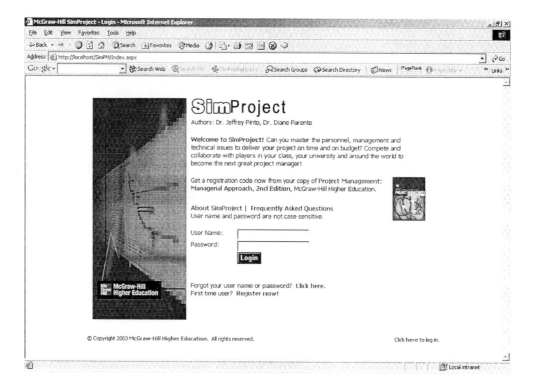

Figure 11 SimProject™ Home Page

2) Enter your User Name and Password into the respective fields. Note that neither the User Name or Password are case sensitive, but you must type them in exactly as you entered them when you registered, including any spaces or other characters.

If you have forgotten your password, see the "Forgot your Password?" section, later in this document.

If you have entered your User Name and Password correctly, you will see the Player Central screen. Otherwise, you will receive a message stating that either your User Name or Password is incorrect or that your account is no longer active.

To Log Out of SimProject™:

1) Click on the "Logout" link in the upper right corner of any screen. Note that this link does not appear if you have not already logged in.

2) You will be returned to the SimProject™ Home Page. See Figure 11

Note that it is always recommended that you log out of SimProject™ immediately upon completing your session.

2.4 Forgot Your Password?

If at any time you cannot remember your SimProject™ password, you can request that it be sent to your email account, which, for security purposes, you were asked to provide when you registered with SimProject™. Enter User Name or Email.

To request your password be sent to you by email:

1) Go to http://www.mhhe.com/simproject . Figure 11 depicts the SimProject™ Home Page.

2) Click on the "Forgot your password? Click here." link. The Retrieve Password screen appears and is depicted in Figure 12.

McGraw-Hill/Irwin

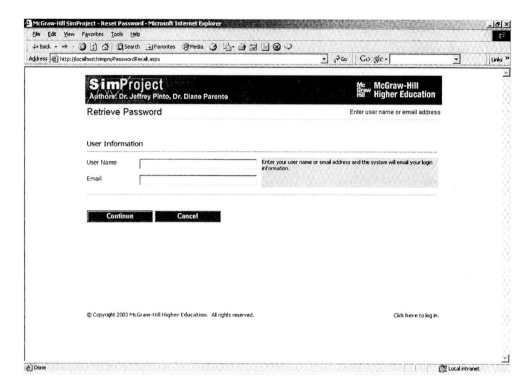

Figure 12 Retrieve Password Screen

3) Enter the User Name or Email Address you entered when you registered with SimProject. If your information matches the information in SimProject™, your password will be emailed to you.

2.5 Managing Teams

There are a number of elements that are necessary to understand about the "Managing Teams" section of the simulation. Because the manner in which you select and maintain your project team has a direct bearing on project performance, it is critical that you clearly understand how resource options are generated and how the selection process works.

64

2.6 Player Central

Once you have logged into the simulation, you will be routed to Player Central. This screen contains the basic information about the simulation, allows you to view most recent period results, make period decisions, view and manage your team profile, and so forth. It also displays the current simulation team rankings (See Figure 13).

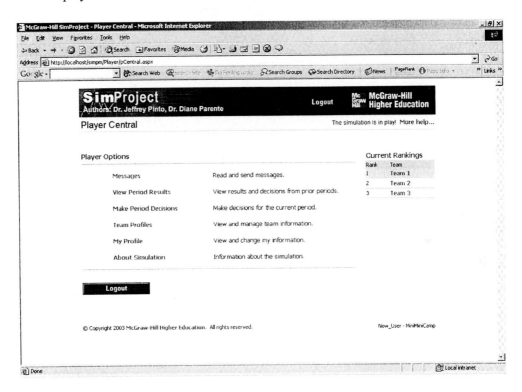

Figure 13 Player Central

2.7 Resources

The main components of the simulation are the resources who will perform tasks, the training they receive, the tasks they will perform, the managerial actions the players make and the random events you assign.

McGraw-Hill/Irwin

This section describes how to view and maintain Resources within the simulation.

2.7.1 View Resources

You can view the resource pool at any time. Just click on the "Resources" link. The resource screen will appear as depicted in Figure 14.

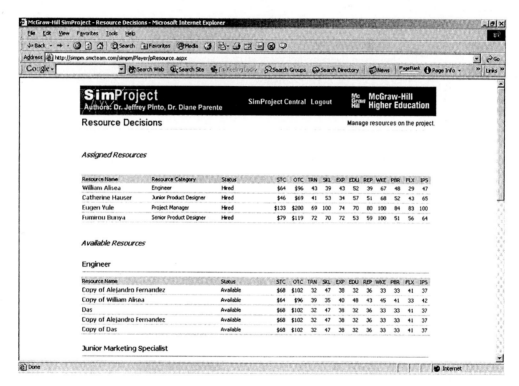

Figure 14 Resources Screen

2.7.2 View Resource Information

To view detailed information about a resource, including skill levels and other attributes, click on the resource's name from the Resources screen. You will see the Resource Detail screen as depicted in Figure 15.

If you select a name, you will find a description of that person, along with some details regarding their skills and any other pertinent information. Figure 15 shows a sample screen description of Anthony Ropar, a junior marketing specialist. Note that all skill levels are evaluated against a perfect 100 score. Therefore, Anthony is rated a 40% for training, 62% for skill level, 40% for experience, and so forth. Finally, the screen lists the standard rate, including overhead costs and minimum rate you could expect to pay for Anthony's services. His overtime rate is also included.

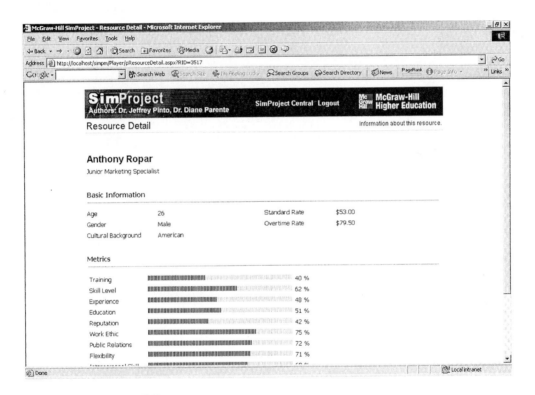

Figure 15 Resource Detail Screen

2.8 Training Catalog

This section describes how to view and maintain Training within the simulation.

2.8.1 View Training

You can view the Training Opportunities at any time. To view the training courses, click on the "Define Training" link. The training screen will appear as depicted in Figure 16.

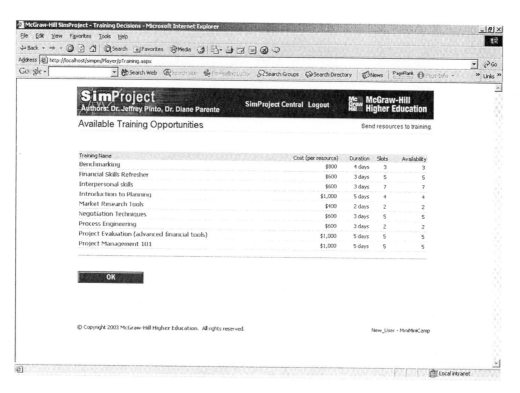

Figure 16 Training Screen

Resources or project team members should be assigned to appropriate training classes. This selection process is shown in Figure 17.

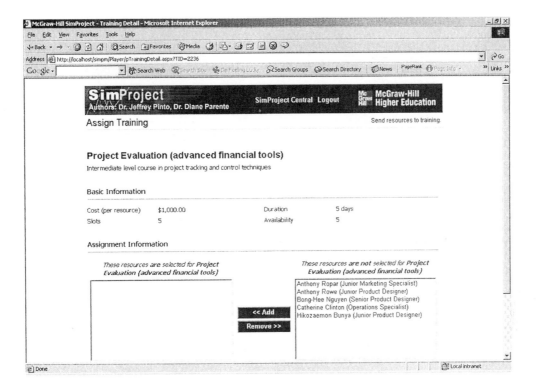

Figure 17 Training Course Assignment

2.8 Work Breakdown Structure (WBS)

This section describes how to view and maintain Work Breakdown Structure (WBS) within the simulation.

2.8.1 View WBS

It is possible to access the tasks that have been assigned for each decision period in the project. Figure 18 shows an example of the tasks that have been identified as needed during period 3 of the simulation. Note that they include the task name, the task group (also referred to as the work package) under which they are classified, the estimated resources hours necessary to complete them, and the number of assigned resources.

McGraw-Hill/Irwin

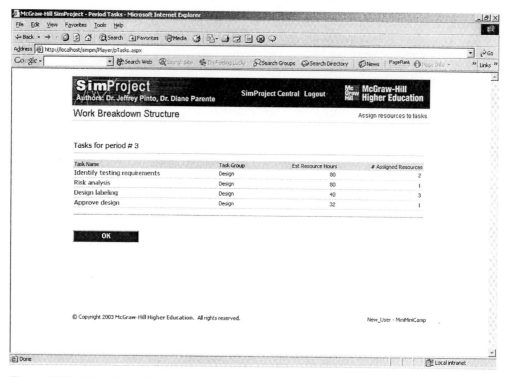

Figure 18 Work Breakdown Structure

2.8.2 View WBS Using MS Project

You can view the MS Project version of the WBS at any time as well. To view the WBS, click on the "Work Breakdown Structure" link. The WBS screen will appear as depicted in Figure 19.

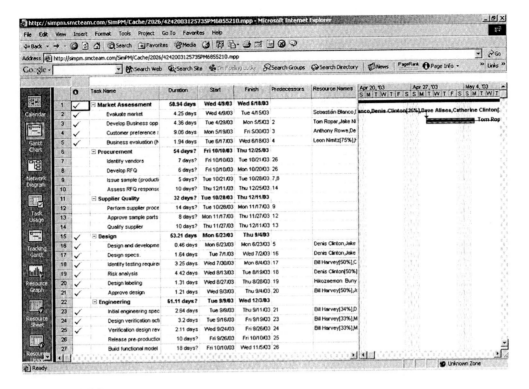

Figure 19 WBS Screen

Using MS Project, it is possible to generate an alternative report on the assignment of resources to project activities during each period. Figure 20 demonstrates an MS Project report screen identifying the activities that have project team resources, the amount of these assignments and the overall effect on the project's resource loading for each decision period.

McGraw-Hill/Irwin

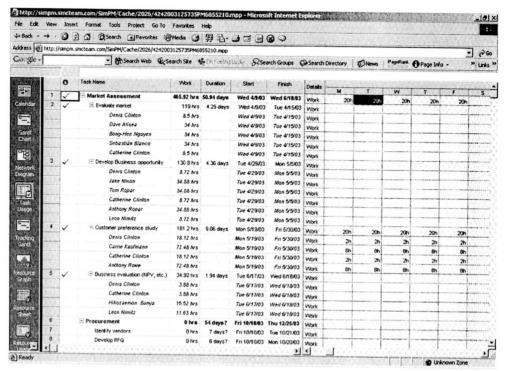

Figure 20 MS Project View of Resource Assignment

2.8.3 View Task & Dependencies

To view detailed information about a Task or its dependencies, click on the task name from the WBS screen. You will see the Task Detail screen as depicted in Figure 21.

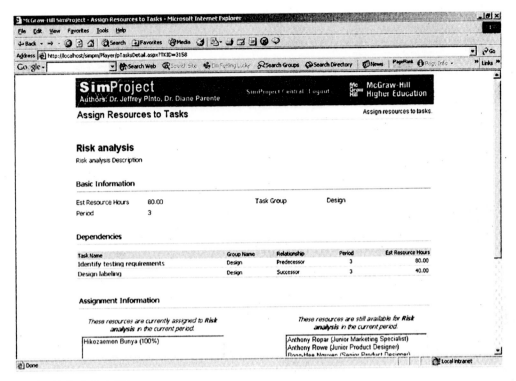

Figure 21 Task Detail Screen

2.9 Managerial Actions

This section describes how to view and maintain Managerial Actions within the simulation.

2.9.1 View Managerial Action

You can view the Managerial Actions at any time. To view the managerial actions, click on the "Managerial Actions" link. The Managerial Actions screen will appear as depicted in Figure 22.

You may also assign managerial actions during the period processing as shown in Figure 23.

McGraw-Hill/Irwin

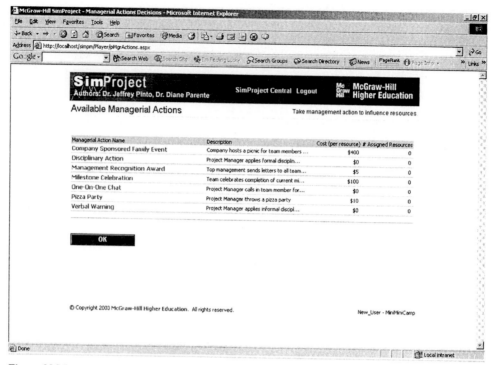

Figure 22 Managerial Actions Screen

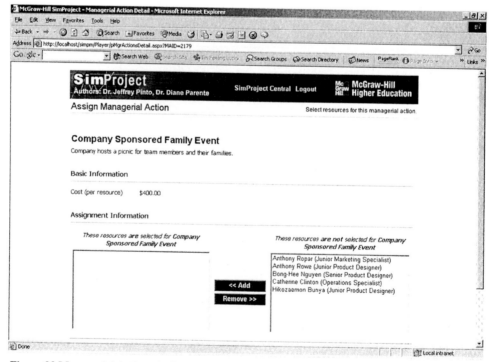

Figure 23 Managerial Actions Assignment

2.10 Period Results

There are a number of results that the simulation teams will generate each decision period. After the instructor has processed the decision round, you will be able to access the Period Results screen (see Figure 24). Each team is ranked in relation to the other simulation teams in terms of their performance on metrics of time, cost, functionality, and stakeholder satisfaction. There is also an overall score that reflects the manner in which the instructor weighted the importance of each of these measures of project performance.

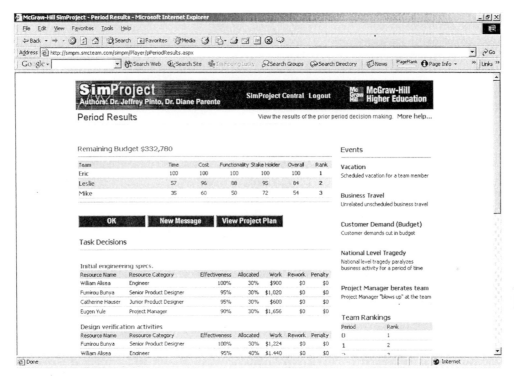

Figure 24 Period Results

Notice also that the Period Results screen gives each of the player teams an updated project budget, as well as a summary of any resource, training, or managerial decisions they made during the most recent period. Finally, any unexpected events that occurred during that period will be displayed on the right side of the screen.

McGraw-Hill/Irwin

2.10.1 Additional Period Reports

Using MS Project, it is possible to generate additional important project status
information following every decision period. Figure 25 displays one such report of the
current status of the project budget, including initial baseline, actual costs and any budget
variances. Because of the direct linkage of the simulation project to MS Project, players
gain real insight into the real-time, on-going effects that their decisions are having on the
status of their simulation project.

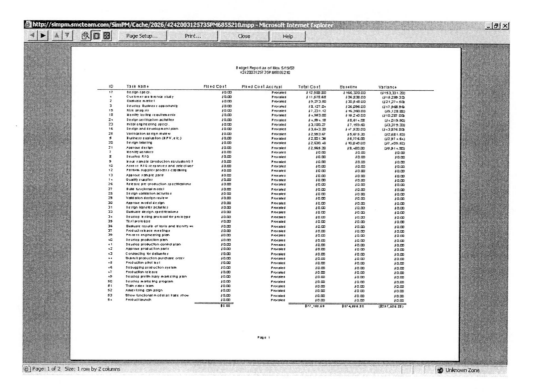

Figure 25 MS Project View (Budget Report)

76

2.11 Playing a Simulation

2.11.1 Overview of Simulation Play

Figure 26 depicts an overview of simulation play and sequence of events. Understanding this flow will help to understand the following sections.

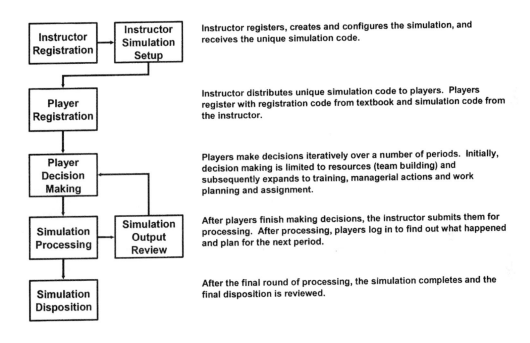

Instructor Registration → Instructor Simulation Setup		Instructor registers, creates and configures the simulation, and receives the unique simulation code.
Player Registration		Instructor distributes unique simulation code to players. Players register with registration code from textbook and simulation code from the instructor.
Player Decision Making		Players make decisions iteratively over a number of periods. Initially, decision making is limited to resources (team building) and subsequently expands to training, managerial actions and work planning and assignment.
Simulation Processing → Simulation Output Review		After players finish making decisions, the instructor submits them for processing. After processing, players log in to find out what happened and plan for the next period.
Simulation Disposition		After the final round of processing, the simulation completes and the final disposition is reviewed.

Figure 26 Simulation Overview

McGraw-Hill/Irwin

2.11 My Profile

The My Profile area is where instructors and players manage their individual profile, including their name and other information, as well as changing their password or email address.

2.11.1 Viewing Your Profile

To view your profile:

1) Log in to SimProject™. See "Logging In and Out of SimProject™".
2) Select **My Profile**.
3) Your profile will be displayed (see Figure 27). Select **Edit Profile** to make changes to your individual information or **Change Password** to change your password.

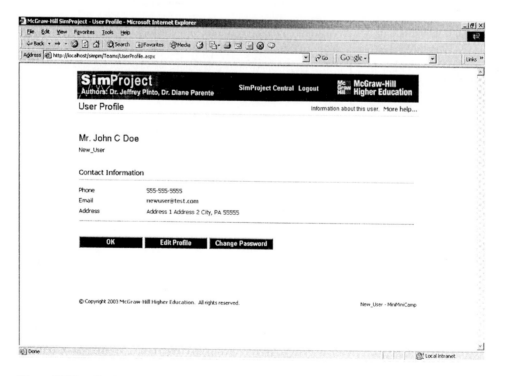

Figure 27 View Profile Screen

2.11.2 Editing Your Profile

To edit your profile:

1) Log in to SimProject™. See "Logging In and Out of SimProject™".

2) Select **My Profile**.

3) Select **Edit Profile**.

4) Your profile will be displayed in an editable form (see Figure 28). Make any changes you would like and click **Save**. To exit without making any changes, press the **Cancel** button.

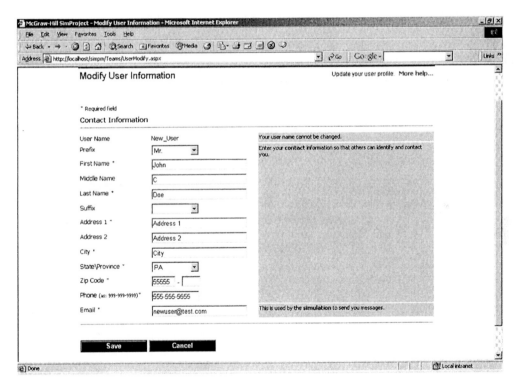

Figure 28 Edit Profile Screen

McGraw-Hill/Irwin

2.11.3 Changing Your Password

To change your password profile:

1) Log in to SimProject™. See "Logging In and Out of SimProject™".
2) Select **My Profile**.
3) Select **Change Password**.
4) The Change Password screen will be displayed (see Figure 29).
5) Enter your **Existing Password** (current).
6) Enter the **New Password** you would like to use.
7) Enter the **New Password** again (confirm) to ensure that you have not mistyped it.
8) Enter a **Password Question** and **Password Answer**. This should be a private question to which only you would know the answer. You may need to provide this later if you forget your password.
9) Click the **Change** button to change your password or the **Cancel** button if you decide not to change your password.

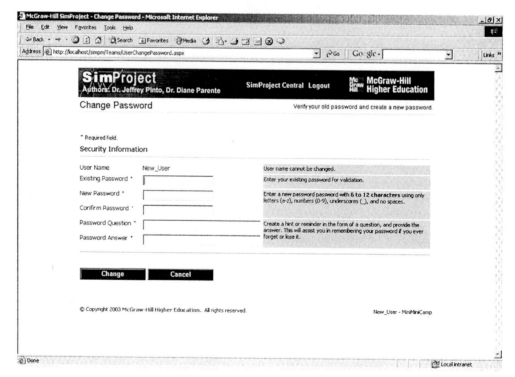

Figure 29 Change Password Screen

2.12 Reading and Posting Messages

The Messages area is a message board where the instructor and players can collaborate on simulation play or class information.

To view messages:

1) Log in to SimProject™. See "Logging In and Out of SimProject™".
2) Select **Messages**.
3) The Messages screen is displayed (see Figure 30).
4) Click on a Subject to view the message (see Figure 31).
5) Post a reply to the message (See Figure 32).
6) Click the **Post Message** button to post a new message (see Figure 33).

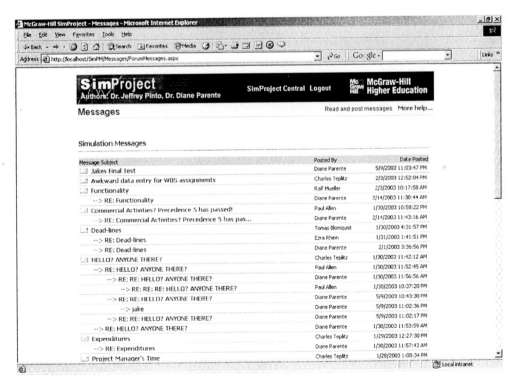

Figure 30 Message Screen

McGraw-Hill/Irwin

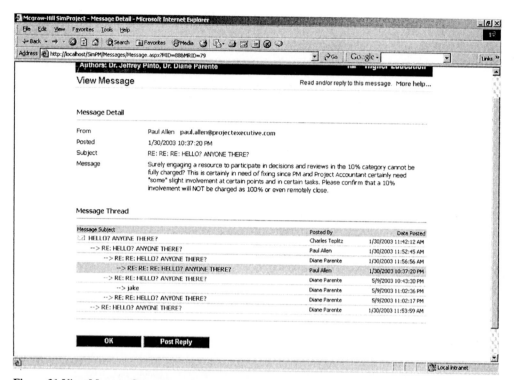

Figure 31 View Message Screen

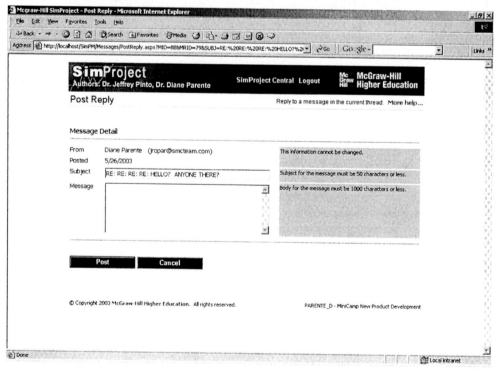

Figure 32 Post Reply Screen

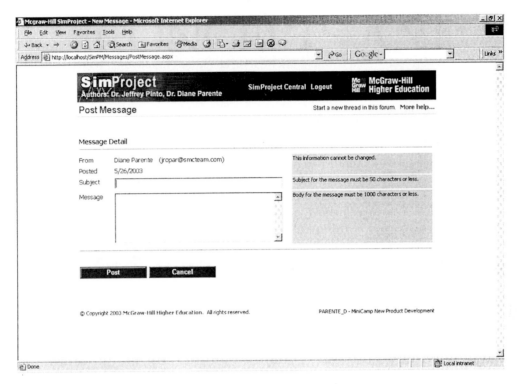

Figure 33 Post Message Screen

2.13 About SimProject™

The About SimProject™ area is where information about the simulation product and McGraw-Hill are located.

To view About SimProject™:

1) From the SimProject™ Home Page, select **About SimProject™.**

2) The About SimProject™ screen is displayed (see Figure 34).

Figure 34 About SimProject™ Screen

2.14 Frequently Asked Questions

The Frequently Asked Questions area, or FAQ, is where the most frequently asked questions and their answers are found.

To view Frequently Asked Questions:

1) From the SimProject™ Home Page, select **Frequently Asked Questions**.

2) The Frequently Asked Questions screen is displayed (see Figure 35).

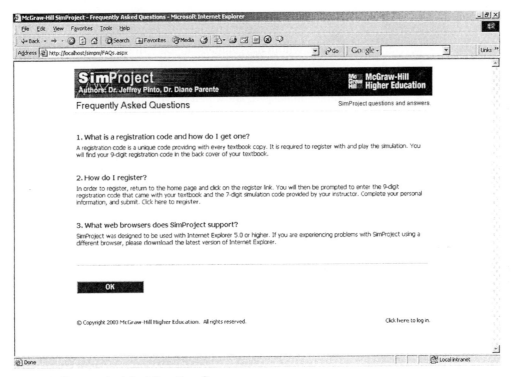

Figure 35 Frequently Asked Questions Screen

FREQUENTLY ASKED QUESTIONS

Most frequently asked questions are available online. This is a partial list only.

Question: What do I do if I forgot my password?

Answer: From the Simulation Home Page, click the "Forgot your username or password? Click here." link. Here you will be prompted to provide your user name or email address. Your password will be emailed to you.

Question: How can I see the project plan, or what I am supposed to do next?

Answer: On several of the screens within the simulation, you will see the "View Project Plan" button. When you click that button, Microsoft Project will come up within the Internet Explorer window. The menu bar will allow you to have full functionality within MS Project.

Question: Do I absolutely **need** MS Project?

Answer: You will not be able to see the project plan without it, which will severely limit your success in the simulation.

Question: The Gantt Chart for my project that appears in Internet Explorer doesn't let me make changes. How can I plan my project?

Answer: When you view your project plan, you may go to File, Save As, and save the file to a floppy disc or a directory on your hard drive. You may then experiment with changes and plan your project including personnel assignments on your own version of the file.

Question: Will the changes I make on my saved version of the project file be uploaded into the next round of SimProject?

Answer: No. You must enter the decisions for each round as discussed in the manual. Uploading is not a feature of this version of the simulation.

Question: Will MS Project 98 work?

Answer: It will work, but many functions were not available in Project 98. We strongly recommend later versions such as Project 2000 or 2002. A 120-day trial version of Microsoft Project 2002 is available free on the CD that accompanies this manual.

Question: I made good decisions. Why did I have such poor results?

Answer: Attempt to critically evaluate your decisions. Did you overassign people? Did you have rework and penalties? Why do you think you had rework? Did you meet the milestone? Why not?

Question: How should I "play" the game?

Answer: Our best advice is that you make decisions that would be logical and also fit the theories that you are learning in Project Management. You will find that if you attempt to "beat" the system, your results will not be very good. If you make decisions that you would make as if you were running this project in the workplace, you will probably do well.

Question: Can I use Netscape for the browser?

Answer: Microsoft Internet Explorer will provide full functionality for SimProject.

Question: How long is a period?

Answer: A period, in terms of time, will be different for every team. At the end of the period, the required tasks will be complete. Each team will take a different amount of time to complete them depending on the skill of the resources and the assignment of resources. If the tasks are not completed with the decisions made, the simulation will assign an appropriate amount of time and money to complete the tasks. If the percent completion does not fall within the range set by the instructor, penalties and rework will be assigned. The end result is that all teams will start the next period of play at the same point in the project and, for the period, will work on the same tasks.